A Biblical
Defense Guide

for Gays, Lesbians and those who love them

Craig Bettend[...]

A meditation of Empowerment Before We Begin

"God you are faithful to all humans, you bore us all, you raised us all, you teach us all, there is not one living on the face of the earth that you have subjected to less than divinity. We pray loving God that you come unto each of us today and instruct us with your words so that as the New Testament shouts, we study to show ourselves approved, a people worthy of your salvation! (The Book of Common Prayer)

Note for Librarians: A cataloguing record for this book is available from Library
and Archives Canada at www.collectionscanada.ca/amicus/index-e.html

ISBN 1-4120-6825-8

*Printed in Victoria, BC, Canada. Printed on paper with minimum 30% recycled fibre.
Trafford's print shop runs on "green energy" from solar, wind and other environmentally-
friendly power sources.*

Offices in Canada, USA, Ireland and UK
This book was published *on-demand* in cooperation with Trafford Publishing.
On-demand publishing is a unique process and service of making a book
available for retail sale to the public taking advantage of on-demand
manufacturing and Internet marketing. On-demand publishing includes
promotions, retail sales, manufacturing, order fulfilment, accounting and
collecting royalties on behalf of the author.

Book sales for North America and international:
Trafford Publishing, 6E–2333 Government St.,
Victoria, BC v8t 4p4 CANADA
phone 250 383 (864 (toll-free 1 888 232 4444)
fax 250 383 6804; email to orders@trafford.com
Book sales in Europe:
Trafford Publishing (UK) Ltd., Enterprise House, Wistaston Road Business Centre,
Wistaston Road, Crewe, Cheshire CW2 7RP UNITED KINGDOM
phone 01270 251 396 (local rate 0845 230 9601)
facsimile 01270 254 983; orders.uk@trafford.com
Order online at:
trafford.com/05-1736

10 9 8 7 6 5

Contents

Preface

I Peter 3:15 offers us "*sanctify Christ as redeemer in your hearts, always being ready to make a defense to everyone who asks you, to give an account for the hope that is in you, with gentleness and reverence.*"

Throughout the history of Christianity countless people have been asked to offer a testimony of their faith in the person of Jesus Christ. Oftentimes the expression of their faith led them to abuse, neglect or even death. Even now, people within today's society who do not fit the established norm are often faced with having to defend their faith expression, as if God couldn't possibly have anything worthwhile to offer others through their testimony. This book is offered up as a testament to the Holy Spirit who calls each of us to share our light, regardless of our warts. I Peter 3:15 is a simple mandate instructing each of us to be ready to defend our faith and is a most excellent way to begin this study.

The evening before I first presented The Biblical Defense Guide as a workshop in Los Angeles, I found myself flipping through the radio dial from one end to the other. I soon happened upon an evangelical fundamentalist broadcast which allegedly focused on family values. The entire time that I listened, a good forty-five minutes, seemed to be a non-stop tirade against Gay and Lesbian people. The program expressed its opinion that those in support of "the Gay agenda," joined feminists and abortion rights organizers who were about to bring American culture and society to the brink of collapse. They even compared the Eagle of the United States of America to that of ancient Rome, juxtaposing the two civilizations. The most agonizing moments of the broadcast came in a segment that dealt with the possibility of Gay parenting. The hosts determined that Gays and Lesbians couldn't possibly parent effectively. That they possessed none of the natural skills necessary to raise children. Soon thereafter a female caller added her comments stating that she was the daughter of a Lesbian Mother. She confirmed for the broadcasters what had previously been said. She lamented her terrible childhood, which she blamed on her Lesbian Mothers influence. She ended the call stating that she was in such agony because she knew that her Lesbian Mother couldn't possibly join her in Heaven.

The woman sobbed as her voice was filled with anguish and pain. This woman more than likely heard much of what she regurgitated from her pastor, or perhaps from other such talk shows. The radio hosts allowed this woman to believe that because her Mother was Lesbian, that there was no hope that they might possibly be reunited in the afterlife. Together they assisted this woman's spirit in breaking even further apart, offering no hope or encouragement in finding some form of common ground between she and her Mother. Malpractice insurance should be mandatory for all of those entering the helping professions, including evangelical fundamentalist talk show hosts. It is my greatest hope that this caller of so long ago, will somehow receive a copy of this book and that it will assist her and her Mother to begin a process of healing and reconciliation.

1

The Sin of Sodom

SODOM AND GOMORRAH is the jumping off point from which many fundamentalist preachers begin their attack on the hearts of the unknowing. This then is where we must begin. First however, one clarifying comment must be made. This being that many preachers use a style of preaching known as "**proof texting**". They begin their sermon preparation with a central idea, going about a process of finding Bible verses that sound convincing to their central argument. They simply plug these verses in, sighting them as they go. Quite often, many such preachers have little understanding of an entire book of the Bible, or of the complexity that it involves. If one can pull a single verse that suits one's immediate needs, like a magician pulling a rabbit from a hat, why they must wonder invest extra time in study?

Our study of the story of Sodom and Gomorrah will begin with a broad background which will assist you in viewing this story in its entirety. The story that is most often cited in relation to the destruction of

Sodom and Gomorrah is found in Genesis, chapter 19, however, we will begin our review in chapter 14.

The Kingdoms of Sodom and Gomorrah were plain states surrounded by hills. Because they were located on open flat land, invaders often attacked them. After one such attack, the King of Assyria ruled both the Kingdoms of Sodom and Gomorrah along with everything else on the open plain for a period of roughly twelve years. For more than a decade, the people of Sodom and Gomorrah paid taxes to the Assyrians, worshiped the gods of the Assyrians and bowed down to the King of the Assyrians. They were a captive people in their own land.

The Fourteenth Chapter illustrates how the former Monarchs of Sodom and Gomorrah finally gained enough courage to mount an attack against their occupiers. A breaking point had been reached and the people decided to no longer pay homage to their captures, regardless of the consequences. Verse ten states that they collectively told the Assyrian King that they were finished paying him taxes. In response the Assyrian King and all of his troops attacked the plains in hopes of destroying the Kingdom's of Sodom and Gomorrah once and for all. As one reads through chapter ten it is obvious that fate did not favor Sodom and Gomorrah, they lost badly, many falling into open tar pits to their gruesome deaths. The Kingdoms of Sodom and Gomorrah lost their bid for independence and once again bowed before Assyrian rule.

The covenant relationship described throughout the Old Testament between God and his people did not begin with Moses as many assume, but with Abraham. This one fact makes Abraham the Father of Judaism and

Christianity collectively. Abraham's nephew, whom he loved very much named Lot, resided in Sodom. Lot and his family were prisoners of the Assyrian occupation. All of Lot's wealth had been taken from them and they lived in abject poverty. When Abraham learned that his nephew was being held against his will he sent out his trained servants, born in his own house, 318 of them. The 318 servants were sent out , ultimately chasing the Assyrians down. The servants of Abraham were not only successful in reuniting Lot and his family with Abraham, but in freeing many of those formerly held by the occupation.

Verse 15 offers a recap of the 318 servants battle plan. "And he divided his forces against them by night, and his servants defeated them and pursued them as far as Hoba which is North of Damascus." Abraham and his 318 men attacked by night while the Assyrians were not on guard, over-running them and liberating the people of Sodom and Gomorrah. In verse 17 the Kings of Sodom and of Salem met Abraham and praised him for his great acts of courage. Abraham wasn't a warlord, he was just a very capable shepherd who happened to have 318 men around who were willing to fight to the death for him. The Kings were overjoyed with their liberation freely offering Abraham all of their possessions, asking only that he leave the people behind to rebuild their homes. In other words they offered Abraham the spoils of war, "take our assets but leave our people." Abraham stunned both Kings by refusing their generous offer, stating that he wouldn't take anything, not even a single thread. Abraham was obviously a man sent by God to accomplish a tremendous act in the history of his people.

To Recap, Sodom and Gomorrah were plain states attacked by the Assyrians, held in captivity for 12 years, they paid lots of taxes. Lot happened to be there. Abraham didn't like the fact that his nephew was held captive, so he attacked the Assyrians, freeing both kingdoms. This is the essential background of the story of Sodom and Gomorrah.

Chapter 18 offers additional background information regarding Abraham. He together with his wife, Sarah, tried for many years to conceive an heir to no avail. They were very old, well into their one hundredth year. They remained faithful to God and were eventually rewarded with the birth of a male child. Chapter 18 verse 20 states, "And the Lord said ,the outcry of Sodom and Gomorrah is indeed great and their sin is exceedingly grave." The story continues with the arrival of three persons in Abraham's encampment one day. Theologians have believed for centuries that two of these visitors were Angels and that the third was actually God. While God was together with the two Angels, and Abraham's family, he exclaimed "The outcry of Sodom and Gomorrah is indeed great and their sin is exceedingly grave." Please take the time to imagine this for a moment. This is God speaking. Sodom and Gomorrah were not good cities, they were wicked in the eyes of God.

A Great Negotiator is born
God continues in verse 21 by saying, " I will go down now and see if they have done entirely according to its outcry. Which has come unto me: and if not, I will know." God has determined that he will send his two Angels to visit the cities who will take careful notes and

return with their final report. Verse 25 further clarifies the spirit of Abraham as he actually enters into a debate with God. Abraham states, " Far be it from thee to do such a thing, to slay the righteous with the wicked, so that the righteous and the wicked are treated alike. Far be it from thee, shall not the judge of all the earth deal justly?" Abraham is afraid that if God sends his Angels to Sodom and that if things turn out the way he already perceives, that God will destroy everyone and everything. Abraham boldly asks God, "If I can find 50 righteous people within the city, then will you spare the whole place on their account?" God thinks it over and agrees, yes if there are 50 righteous people living there, the city will be spared for their account. Abraham asks again, if there are 45 righteous people in all of Sodom will you spare it?" Again, God agrees.

Verse 28 emphasizes that Abraham had just begun his serious negotiating. "How about 40?" Yes, if there are 40 righteous people in all of Sodom, it will be spared," says God. Abraham continues, 30?, yes 30. 20?, yes 20. Abraham senses his negotiating going very well and drops down all the way to 10. God concedes that for 10 righteous people, he will not destroy Sodom. As one reads this story it is good to keep in mind that the whole of Christianity believes God to be all powerful and all knowing. God did not need to send his emissary Angels down to Sodom in order to determine their level of sin. God already knew because God knows all--nowhere in Christianity is this one central tenant disputed. Please continue to bear this in mind as we continue with this story.

We continue with the 19th chapter, this being the chapter where most fundamentalists begin telling their account of Sodom and Gomorrah. Verse one states that the two Angels arrived in Sodom in the evening as Lot was sitting at the entrance gate of the city. Lot rose to meet the Angels, only recognizing that they were strangers approaching the city at nightfall. Lot stated "Now behold my Lords, please turn aside into your servants house and spend the night, wash your feet, so that you may rise early in the morning and go your way." The Angels politely refused stating that they would rather stay the night in the village square. Lot, being of a good family and having full knowledge of the rite of hospitality continued to persuade the travelers to lodge with his family for the night. We are told that the strangers eventually agreed to stay in Lot's home and that he in turn prepared unleavened bread for them to eat. After dinner, before they laid down (before they began to sleep) we are told that the men of the city surrounded the house, both young and old and from every quarter. Lot, his family and their guests had just finished dinner and were beginning to settle in for the night as their home was surrounded by their neighbors. The Scripture states that "all of the men of the village surrounded the house" however it is historically believed that "men" was an all encompassing description of "people" during this time. Women at that time had achieved no social standing and were still largely considered to be the property of men. All of the people of Sodom surrounded the house and they called out "where are the men who came to you tonight?"

The second statement they made seemed quite logical "bring them out so that we may know them." In today's terms you could envision their practical concerns. The strangers had entered the city at nightfall, no one from immigration was on hand to stamp their passports, they just arrived and were swept away to safety in Lots home.

We are told that Lot was the first at the door, acting calmly asking those gathered to act more hospitably. After a time and for his own reasons, Lot offers his two daughters to the crowd, if they will only disperse and leave his guests alone. I will discuss his possible motivations for this at a later point. Lot makes a plea to the mob, "Do nothing to these men as they came under the shelter of my roof." The neighbors gathered reminded Lot that he came to their city as an alien himself and now he was already acting like a judge. Lot wasn't even a citizen and he was telling the officials of the city, gathering outside his home which rules to enforce. We are told that once the crowd pressed Lot at the door, threatening to treat him badly that the Angels reached out pulling Lot back into the house, slamming the door. The Angels struck each of those in the crowd who refused to disband with blindness. We are told that they all wearied themselves trying to find an exit. The citizens surrounding Lots house, who had trespassed by entering his dwelling were struck blind. This is an interesting action chosen by the mighty Angels who could have just as easily struck them dead. The Angels then instructed Lot to gather up his family and prepare to make a hasty exit. They had determined that the city would be destroyed as they departed. The Angels stated that " the outcry has been so great against the Lord and that the Lord had sent them to destroy the City." They have just recited Gods statement from back in Chapter 18, verse 20, "the outcry has been great and that their sin is exceedingly grave." The field assessment was in, Sodom was toast.

Lot wasn't able to convince all of his relatives to depart quickly, the Angels actually grabbed the hands of his Wife and Daughters, pulling them from the city. The twenty-fifth verse states "And he threw those cities and all the valley and all of the inhabitants of the cities and all that had grown, to the ground." This description is very familiar to those of us living in California. The thunderous rage of an earthquake suddenly throws all that was built up, to the ground. The twenty fourth and twenty fifth verses state that God rained on Sodom and Gomorrah with brimstone and fire from the heavens. This too sounds familiar by today's understanding, a volcanic eruption.

When this story is told by the biblical literalists (fundamentalists) one is asked to believe that God destroyed Sodom and Gomorrah because the men of Sodom broke into Lots house to force the Angels into having sex with them. Sadly enough I must state that the majority of Bibles produced in the last ten years are written to support this fundamentalist interpretation. The majority of the Bible publishing companies have been purchased by the rabidly fundamentalist fringe in their attempt to control the message of the Scripture for generations to come.

Based on the reading of the 19th chapter of Genesis one can come to four possible conclusions as to why Sodom and Gomorrah were destroyed. The first being that the cities were destroyed for general wickedness, which had prompted God to send his Angels to investigate in the first place. If we refer back to Genesis 18 verse 20 and Genesis 19 verse 13 we see quit clearly that God in his all knowing way knew that these were wicked cities. The second possibility is that the cities were destroyed because the people tried to gang rape the Angels in an act of subordinating them to their rule. The third possibility is that the cities were destroyed because the men that gathered outside the house wanted to have homosexual sexual relations with the Angels. (Boswell, 1980, p.93)

The fundamentalists seem to wind number two and three together although they are different subjects all together. In Jewish tradition the act of rape was different from the act of homosexual intercourse. It was customary during this era for a conquering General or Commander to plunder a city then gather their adversaries (opposing rulers, generals, etc.) into the town square where they would be made to endure rape at the hand of the conquerors. The idea of equality of the sexes was eons away and the thought of making a male authority figure subordinate in a sex act was to degrade him beyond belief. The difference between male rape of males and homosexual intercourse must be stated clearly, a historical distinction between the two has been understood by scholars for centuries.

If therefore the fundamentalists have it half right, it may be in the male rape scenario. It would fit the historical and cultural norm as an "outside possibility" , although not as a primary explanation.

Since 1955, modern scholarship has favored a fourth interpretation. The fourth interpretation states that the cities were destroyed for inhospitable treatment of visitors sent by God. The fourth possibility has gained increased favor emphasizing that the sexual overtones in the story are minor if at all present and that the true sin of Sodom was treating strangers inhospitably. (Boswell, 1980, p. 93)

The act of inhospitality may seem commonplace or even ordinary in our day. I tend to believe that all of us come in contact with rude behavior almost daily. It seems to have become an accepted norm within our society. Rudeness, however is not the same as inhospitality. During the time that the Bible was written, daily survival was very difficult. If one made a wrong turn in a foreign land, it could easily lead to starvation or death by the elements. For this reason a *code of conduct* was established in many cultures of the time in which hospitality was recognized as the paramount societal behavior. If a stranger came to you thirsty, you offered him drink because one day you may be entirely out of water and nearly dead due to extreme heat and dehydration. If a stranger came to you hungry, you gave him food, for the same reasons. People actually opened their homes to strangers who were lost or who had too far to travel in order to reach their own homes by nightfall. All of this seems strange in our current day, yet this was a lynch pin in the survival of all people for quit some time.

Lot's difficulties occurred that night due to his intense honor of these rites of hospitality. He met the strangers at the city gates just prior to nightfall. He encouraged them to join his family for dinner, rest and bathe. Lot was acting in accordance with his Hebrew tradition. Lot however failed to remember that he himself was a foreigner in this land.

Lot invited strangers into the city limits at nightfall without giving any sort of notification to the town elders. The concept of entertaining strangers within the city walls after nightfall without proper notification/registration was a probable violation of the law within his new home town. The concept of the people coming to his house after nightfall demanding that the strangers be brought out so that they may "know them" seems to be a rational request.

The phrase "to know" them is where the biblical literalist complicates this very simple story. The Hebrew verb "to know" used in Genesis 19:5 is spelled YADHA. YADHA is used within 943 verses of the Old Testament as found in the King James version of the Bible. Out of 943 times biblical scholars believe that the word YADHA may have had a sexual connotation in 10 cases. Within these 10 cases YADHA is known to mean **sexual relations between a man and his wife**, this is also very important. (McNeill, 1993 p.43) Bring them out so that we may "know them" misses the target of sexual misconduct because clearly none of the Angels were married to any of the towns people. There are rare accounts within scripture of Angels in fact having sexual relations, which I know is a mind bender. These accounts will also be explored in detail within this book because the biblical literalists (fundamentalists) have recently been assigning these few acts as homosexual relations as well.

2

What About Gibeah?
Sodom's twin Sister

The most important fact of the previous chapter was found in Genesis 18:20, "And the Lord said the outcry in Sodom and Gomorrah is indeed great and their sin is exceedingly grave, I will go down and see if they have done entirely according to its outcry which has come to me and if not I will know."

God, is ascribed omnipotent, omniscient, all knowing power by all Christian traditions. Furthermore, to say that God did not know exactly what was occurring in the cities of Sodom and Gomorrah prior to the visit of the Angels, would strip God of this essential Christian doctrine. In so saying, one would actually be speaking against Scripture and tradition. Stating that God is not all knowing would be paramount to heresy in every single Christian tradition. It would be far more fitting to say that God sent the Angels to Sodom in order to experience and confirm that which God already knew, first hand. The inhospitable treatment of these cities, in so much as they were treated so horrendously by the general public, being pulled from a place of safety and comfort out into the street in the middle of the night acted as a final confirmation.

Genesis 19:13 states that the Angels tell Lot and his immediate family to quickly gather what they need and to evacuate the city at once. This is a direct confirmation of what God had earlier stated in Chapter 18, "For we are about to destroy this place because the outcry has become so great before the Lord." The central point of importance is that the Angels were sent to destroy the city and that the determination had been previously made by the all knowing God.

Impassioned fundamentalist preachers would have one believe that those poor Angels were sent to Sodom and that the vile, horrible homosexuals wanted to rip them from that house and have their sexually deviant way with them. This is why God destroyed Sodom, they will say. One final review of Genesis 19:4 is in order. "Before they lay down, the men of the city (remembering that women bore no role in community authority at this point in history) surrounded the house, both young and old, all people from every quarter." Every quarter of the city speaks to neighborhoods of the city. One only need visit New Orleans to hear areas and neighborhoods still referred to as quarters. This verse states that people from every neighborhood (quarter) of the city surrounded the house that night. I would like you to think of all of the people in any neighborhood that you have ever lived. In Los Angeles that would take a lot of concentration as people from all ends of the globe have found a home there. Many of the cities of the Old Testament era were similarly melting pots or salad bowls of culture and diversity. If we put the fundamentalists argument into a logical context it bears absolutely no sense at all. There has never been a City, a State, a Province or a Country at anytime in the history of humankind that has ever been exclusively homosexual. The concept of an exclusively homosexual community defies all logic, as homosexual persons rarely bare offspring.

The context of any community in the pre-Christian era being exclusively homosexual is ridiculous. A cities strength and power rested in its number of residents. There has never been an exclusively homosexual civilization, ever!

Please recall that a few verses down, Lot offers his Daughters to those people surrounding the house as a form of appeasement. If we use the simplest common sense it isn't even logical to consider that homosexual rapists would desire female victims. Lot obviously knew some of his neighbors, if not all of them he certainly knew that some may desire the offer of his daughters. If in fact the fundamentalists claim, "that sexual perversion" was the sin of Sodom and that the people surrounding the house were demanding sex, Lot sending his daughters out assuming that they had a subordinate place in society may be a way of saying, "I'm protecting these visitors even at the cost of my own family". Two females in place of the visiting Angels is not an offer conducive to reducing the tension surrounding Lots home that night. Neither is it conducive to the Old Testament epic to scape- goat a people misunderstood and despised by the majority. This view is neither enlightened, nor Christian. It merely points the finger at a small percentage of the population, assigning the blame of the story to a few, rather than accepting responsibility as an entire culture or community. This is an often used propaganda tactic which the dominate culture will use to scape-goat a minority. Hitler used it very much to his advantage in Germany. Others too have employed its wicked tenants. Blame a smaller sub-population for ones plight and the majority need not explore its own issues. God spared Lot and his daughters from certain destruction. The fundamentalists would like us to ignore the fulfilling of the rite of hospitality and would prefer to blame the destruction of both cities on the sexual lusts of the villagers.

Chapter 19:33-36 takes up after Lot and his daughters have left the city fleeing to safety. Lots wife who began the journey with them failed to listen to the warning not to look back at the city, turning into a pillar of salt. The loss of Lots wife is important because it sets the stage for a part of the story overlooked by the majority of fundamentalist preachers. Once evening had come and they had made camp we read the following, "So they made their Father drink wine that night and the first born went in and lay with her Father, and he did not know when she lay down or when she arose." There isn't any argument with the facts of this verse from any literate Christian group or believer. Lot and his daughters drank wine and his eldest daughter slept with her father that night. Unlike the confusion over YADHA, "to know", no such confusion exists here. Christendom as a whole acknowledges that the act of sexual intercourse between Father ad Daughter (incest) occurred that night and that it is documented in this verse. Verse 34 continues "And it came about on the morrow in the morning, that the first born said to the younger, behold

I lay last night with my Father, let us make him drink wine tonight also, then you go in and lay with him, that we may preserve our family." Verse 35 continues "So they made their Father drink wine that night also and the younger arose and lay down with him and he did not know when she lay down or she arose." In other words Lot got drunk and each daughter had sexual intercourse with him. Once again, if the fundamentalists claim that Sodom and Gomorrah were destroyed because of "wicked sexual perversion", I would refer them to this forgotten moment of the Sodom saga. On the very evening of their deliverance out of the city, just hours after their salvation from certain destruction, both Lot and his daughters committed the horrendous sin of incest. INCEST was forbidden without doubt in all circles of Judaic custom. Those participating in this act often met a violent end by the hands of those keeping the Laws of Moses. I am surprised by how many fundamentalists miss calling down the wrath of Leviticus 20:14 upon Lot for his sin. Please take a moment and consider all of those destroyed in the Cities of Sodom and Gomorrah. If Sodom was destroyed because its male population wanted to rape or just have homosexual sex with the Angels, why were so many destroyed? Why the Women, the children, the animals? Why was the city of Gomorrah thrown into the fire if the sin that brought them to a sure destruction occurred in the city next door, having nothing to do with this one act themselves? In the minds of most scholars today the answer as to why Sodom and Gomorrah were destroyed lies elsewhere, the old "blame it on the Gays" just doesn't work once you've read the entire story preserved to this day in Scripture.

Worthless fellows & choice men

Sodom and Gomorrah is widely used as a justification for the marginalization of those within the Lesbigay community. If asked, most people would confirm that they had heard the tale of Sodom and Gomorrah but how about the story of Gibeah?

In the Book of Judges Chapter 19, which at first seems to be quite a coincidence, (Sodom's story being in Genesis Chapter 19) we find the very similar account of the city of Gibeah. We begin this story at Judges 19:16; "Then behold an old man was coming out of the field from his work at evening, now the man was from the hill country of Efrian and he was staying in Gibeah, but the men of the place were Benjaminites" which is to say that this man was a foreigner who resided in Gibeah, just as Lot was a foreigner who lived in Sodom. "And he lifted up his eyes and saw the traveler in the open square of the city and the old man said, where are you going and where do you come from?" These are strikingly similar words used by Lot to the Angeles in Genesis as he met them in the city square by the gate. "And he said to him, we are passing from Bethlehem and Judea to the remote part of the hill country of Efrian, for I am from there and I went to Bethlehem and Judea but I am now going to my home and no man will take me into his house."

Again, when a stranger in need asks for help in this time and culture, you accept them in the simple rite of hospitality. "Yet there is both straw and fodder for our donkeys and also bread and wine for me, your maid-servant and a young man who is with your servants, there is no lack of anything", he is saying that in this one city there seems to be no lack of anything, yet no one will take him in for the night. "And the old man said, peace to you, only let me take care of your needs, however, do not spend the night in the open square." Just as Lot tells the Angels to come home with him and asks them not to spend the night in the open square, the old man encourages the strangers in the same words, in the same way. "So he took them to his house and gave the donkeys food and they washed their feet and ate and drank." The next verse follows the Genesis 19:22 verbatim. "While they were making merry, behold the men of the city, certain worthless fellows surrounded the house, pounding on the door saying to the owner of the house, bring the man out who came into your house so that we may know him."

Then the owner of the house went out to meet them and said "No my fellows please do not act so wickedly, since this man has come into my house, do not commit this act of folly." These are strikingly similar words to those used by Lot to his crowd. (Boswell, 1980, p.95) Verse 24 continues in a remarkably similar way "Here's my virgin daughter and his concubine (wife), ravish them and do to them whatever you must, but do not commit such an act of folly against this man." The old man reiterates Lots offering to the crowd, offering the two females within his household to the crowd in order to insure the safety of his guest. We read on to see "But the men would not listen to him, so they seized his concubine and brought her out" raping and abusing her until morning light. In the case of Gibeah, the crowd submits to the hosts urges , taking their vengeance out on the concubine, more than likely in plain view in order to attest their control over the town.

As we follow the chapter, the house guest returns to

his home, he is a Levite , a member of a priestly order and he is very upset by the mobs actions. He demands that the sin of inhospitality be punished Judges 20:5; "He gave the account of the men in Gibeah saying, when the men of Gibeah rose against me and surrounded the house at night intending to kill me, instead they ravished my concubine (wife) so that she died." He states that they intended to kill him (not have sex with him, or rape him) and that they killed his wife after multiple rapes. The Levite is so distressed that his wife is dead that he cuts her body up into many pieces sending them to the various camps of Israelites to anger them, hoping to evoke their emotion and receive their assistance. The man was offering them a Macomb calling card, here's my dead wife, come fight with me against the murderous heathens of Gibeah.

The calling card worked very well. Scripture recalls that "The people of Israel (minus the Benjaminites who were pledged to defend Gibeah) rose as if one man" saying, we will not go home, we will go directly into battle in order to vindicate this injustice. The fifteenth verse shows us the outrageous power at the hand of the maligned Levite "And from the cities on that day the sons of Benjamin were numbered 25,100 who drew their swords combining their forces along with 700 choice men of Gibeah. The men of Israel took count, without Benjamin they numbered 400,000. Prior to the attack the Israelites sent a message to the defending Benjaminites stating that "they must turn over the scoundrels of Gibeah so that they may be put to death in order to banish their wickedness from Israel". We are told that the Benjaminites would not listen to their brother Israelites. The people of Gibeah and their defending allies the Benjaminites were not to be taken lightly. Scripture recounts that on the first day of battle, the Benjaminite-Gibeah force, who were far out numbered , killed 22,000 Israelites, sending them into a state of retreat and panic. On the second day of fighting the Benjaminite-Gibeah force again assaulted the Israelites killing another 18,000. The elders went to God on that night, praying along with Aaron at the Ark of the Covenant, asking if they should again wage an attack against their small but mighty foe. On the third day and after the Israelites received consolation from God himself, they met the Benjaminite-Gibeah forces, surprising them and destroying their entire army, 25,100 men.

The Benjaminite-Gibeah forces were later described as "choice men who could kill a rabbit with a single stone and who could handle a sword with either hand". These were extremely powerful adversaries as demonstrated in the first two days of battle.

The defeat of Gibeah at the hands of the Israelites served as God's destruction of an evil people, just as the fire and brimstone destruction of Sodom and Gomorrah had. Both inhabitants of Sodom and Gibeah met with destruction because of cruel, inhumane treatment of strangers, in direct violation of the laws of hospitality. In the story of Sodom the people wanted "to know" the visitors who had entered after dusk. In Gibeah the Levite makes it clear that they wanted to "kill" him. If we were to place the misused logic of the fundamentalists onto Gibeah (destruction due to homosexual relations) that has been placed on Sodom, it just wouldn't work. The story of Gibeah, although little known has been well preserved with lots of details of the persons involved. History and numerous re-writes of the account of Sodom has not been as generous. There has been a direct, purposeful ,cultural attempt over the past thirty years to simply misclassify the story of Sodom as God's vengeance against a homosexual minority. The story of Gibeah did not suit their needs. The clear recollection of the story, its characters and eventual battles did not lend itself to their purposeful re-tooling. This is why Gibeah was more problematic to alter. If Gibeah had also been a Homosexual city as was Sodom, why were their 700 warriors so strong? How could they have been among the best of the best?, the special forces or the Green Berets? And if they were in fact homosexuals, as those in Sodom were alleged, how were they able to employ the willing assistance of the Benjaminites who were willing to be outnumbered 16 to 1 in battle? Why were the Benjaminites, also Israelites themselves, willing to cause a civil war among their own people in order to defend a hated minority? No, they must have thought to themselves, Gibeah would take far too much revision. Sodom on the other hand has this little verse, "bring them out so that we may know them". It is far easier to change "to know" into "rape in a homosexual manner" in the minds of future generations of Christian children than it would be to revise the little read, hard to find and very detailed story of Gibeah!

Although I feel as if I have exhausted the story of Sodom, I would like to roll back the story one more time in order to explain the rite of hospitality clearly. Going back to Genesis the 18th chapter, God and the two Angels first appear to Abraham to discuss what they were planning for Sodom. "So when he lifted up his eyes and looked, he beheld three men, they were standing opposite of him and when he saw them he ran from the tent to meet them, bowing himself to the earth." Please keep in mind that Abraham had no idea that the three strangers were God and two Angels.

Verses 4 through 8 "Please let a little water be brought and wash your feet and rest yourself under the tree and I will bring bread to you that you may refresh yourselves, after that you may go on, since you have visited your servant, and *they said* " so do as you have said." So Abraham hurried into the tent to Sarah his wife saying "Quickly prepare three measures of fine flower, knead it and bake it into bread cakes. Abraham then ran to his herd and took a tender choice calf and he gave it to the servant and he prepared it. He took curds and milk and the calf which he had prepared and placed it before them, standing beside them under the tree while they ate." I would like you to re-read this paragraph and these verses prior to reading on. I would ask you what your reflections of Abraham's actions appear to be most like in our own modern day culture.

It is my opinion and that of many learned scholars that Abraham was organizing a menu. He greeted his guests (although they were total strangers) with a bow. He brought them quick refreshment, water for thirst and for cleaning up. He sat them comfortably under a shady tree while he continued to put together that days menu. A choice calf, milk curd and bread cakes, no expense was spared. Note that the Scriptures do not say he pulled yesterdays left-overs out of the fridge. He picked the choicest items from his agricultural inventory presenting them humbly to his guests. The finest things were reserved for guests, even for strangers.

In retrospect a fundamentalist may say, God certainly didn't destroy Sodom because the people were rude. Most people living today in Western cultures, many of which are rude themselves, would more than likely agree. The Sin of inhospitality as found in the book of Genesis and then reflected again in the book of Judges was such a cultural taboo that the authors of Genesis went to great lengths to spell out the many steps that Abraham took in receiving his guests. Hospitality in that era was considered a sacred act. It was an act with Sacramental value, so much so that it became an integral part of Mosaic Law. I would like to bring this chapter to a close by reviewing four other Scriptural accounts of the importance of the rite of hospitality.

Exodus 22:21, And you shall not wrong a stranger or oppress him, since you yourselves know the feelings of a stranger, for you also were strangers in the land of Egypt."

Exodus 23:9, And you shall not oppress a stranger, since you yourselves know the feelings of a stranger for you also were strangers in the land of Egypt." This must have been written to insure that if it was missed the first time in Chapter 22, that it would be reviewed in Chapter 23.

Deuteronomy 10:17-19, For the Lord your God, is God of Gods and Lord of Lords, the great, the mighty and the awesome God who does not show partiality nor take a bribe. God executes justice for the orphan and the widow and shows God's love for the alien (stranger) by giving the alien food and clothing. So show your love for the alien, or stranger for you were strangers in the land of Egypt.

Deuteronomy 24:17, You shall not pervert the justice due an alien, or an orphan or take a widow's garment (property) in pledge." In other words, you shouldn't take an oath and collateral from a disadvantaged person.

The Early Church Fathers including Oriegan and St. Ambrose made it clear that Sodom's sin was the sin of inhospitality. They both thought that hateful, ungrateful inhospitality was the reason for Sodom's destruction.

The New Jerusalem Bible that can be purchased at any bookstore was originally published as the Jerusalem Bible in 1966. During the early editions of this work a footnote appeared below the story of Sodom and Gomorrah stating that "the underlying story is a horror of the double offense of their behavior against the Angels and the breach of the Law of Hospitality." Latter editions of this work no longer make reference to this footnote, because it no longer exists. It has conveniently disappeared in more recent editions. The fundamentalists have worked hard to first, purchase almost all of the publishing houses currently printing Bibles and second, make footnote paragraphs like the one above disappear from sight. The next generation of Christian youth is likely to never question Bible stories presented to them. They have been neatly repackaged complete with numerous omissions that may have once caused one to search for truth.

3

Joshua fought
the battle at Jericho

Within the last chapter we discussed the city of Gibeah, comparing its story to that of Sodom and Gomorrah. We found that the two stories shared striking similarities so much so that they may be a retelling of the same story through different cultural perspectives. We concluded the study of Gibeah by outlining the absolute importance of the Rite of Hospitality within the cultural , religious and societal constructs of the day. We also alluded to other portions of the Bible which further demonstrated the great importance of the Rite of hospitality.

I would like to begin this study by further referencing the importance of the Rite of Hospitality found within Old Testament scripture. This Rite is well demonstrated within the book of Joshua chapter six. For reason of quick reference I will offer the following background information of this story. Jericho was a city that was completely destroyed by God which is our thread of connection, weaving itself through Sodom, Gibeah and now Jericho. God did not use fire and brimstone to take down Jericho as was used in Sodom. Once again as in the Gibeah story, God inspired the righteous to take up arms against the unrighteous, thus completing God's judgment.

The old Sunday school song "Joshua fought the battle at Jericho and the walls came tumbling down" is the only lasting recollection of this event for many Christians. Chapter 6 begins with God outlining Joshua's attack strategy. God gave Joshua explicit direction on how to approach the city and how to topple its king. God also directed that the Ark of the Covenant along with its seven attending priests be involved. Joshua did as directed and on the seventh day the cities walls collapsed and all within the town was delivered to them. The Scripture seems to intimate that all lives of those living within Jericho should be forfeited and that only Rahab the harlot and her family be spared. Joshua 6:17, "And the city shall be under the ban, it and all that is in it belongs to the Lord , only Rahab the harlot and all that are with her in the house shall live, because she hid the messengers who we sent."

This is an extraordinary story for several reasons. First it speaks of the utter brutality of taking a city and killing all of its inhabitants. Second, the only person deemed worthy of exception is a local prostitute. This is truly an unbelievable exception. Prostitutes held absolutely no warm spot in the hearts of the Israelites. They were despised and held to the lowest rung of the societal ladder. Yet in the story of Joshua taking the city of Jericho it is Rahab the prostitute and her family members that are allowed to live. Rahab and her family survived. The reason for this puzzling outcome, this lottery of the living becomes clear as we explore the story in greater depth.

Joshua like all good generals decided to send his special forces into the city prior to his attack in order to access his enemies readiness. During their undercover excursion the men of Joshua's exploratory team fell into some danger and were in jeopardy of being exposed. Enter Rahab, a simple town prostitute who put the best interest of herself, her city and all of its inhabitants to the side, taking in these strangers, offering them hospitality and refuge.

Livestock 0 Hookers 1

Joshua 6:21 "And they utterly destroyed everything in the city, both man and woman, both young and old, and ox , sheep and donkey with the edge of he sword." Not only were all of the human inhabitants of the city put to death, so were the livestock a valuable commodity. Joshua 6:22 "And Joshua said to the two men who had spied out the land, go into the harlot's house and bring the woman and all she has out of there as you have sworn." Joshua was insuring that Rahab, her family and her possessions made it to safety while all else was leveled.

The Law of Moses was very clear when dealing with sexual impurity. Sexual impurity in all forms was strictly prohibited. Sexual uncleanliness in all forms was outlawed within these cultural and religious provisions. It only takes one look at Genesis 38:24-25 to determine the prevailing attitude of the time towards prostitutes, "Your daughter-in-law has played the harlot; furthermore she is pregnant, as a result of her misconduct." "Take her outside and burn her" said Judah. In this context the person of Rahab must be considered. She was considered among the lowliest of sinners. She continued as a prostitute even knowing that its religious and cultural taboo was so stringent. Joshua doesn't seem to feel warmly toward her, addressing her only as "the harlot".

It is in this context that a brilliant light must shine on the story of Sodom. The sparing of Rahab, a village prostitute, one who broke the Laws of Moses daily in her secular career was the only one spared. The question must be asked and asked boldly. Why would God spare a harlot from death, a self described sexual pervert while destroying an entire civilization in Sodom for the offense of sexual perversion? When these two stories are compared they offer two interesting insights. The first of which is that Sodom was not destroyed for the sin of sexual perversion. The story of a sexual pervert, Rahab being spared while all around her are slaughtered demonstrates this clearly. The argument of Sodom being destroyed for sexual perversion holds no water when compared to this story in Joshua chapter six. Secondly what does measure up is that Rahab was spared for offering hospitality to strangers, thus fulfilling the rite of hospitality and that Sodom acting totally inhospitable to its strangers broke that rite without doubt.

When Sodom, Gibeah and Jericho are all considered as a whole, sexual perversion plays no active role in their destructions. A serious student of Scripture must search for another compelling reason that is consistent in all three stories. The one pervading reason, consistent in all three stories is the Rite of Hospitality. Looking back to Gibeah for one last time a footnote also appeared within the Jerusalem Bible below Judges 19. "It is the violation of the sacred rite of hospitality which is considered a grave infamy." The Jerusalem Bible that took more scholarly talent to compile since any work since the King James version stated clearly that Gibeah was destroyed for the inhospitable treatment of strangers in their care. Sadly, it must be stated that if you check Judges 19 in the New Jerusalem Bible, this footnote has also disappeared. The sin of omission is something which the fundamentalists will undoubtedly answer for in the afterlife.

4

Creative Literalism and New Testament Revisionism

The Rt. Rev. John S. Spong, former Bishop of Newark, New Jersey of the Episcopal Church USA set off a firestorm in 1992 with the publication of his book, Rescuing the Bible from Fundamentalism. His defense of a spirituality minus the mindless literalism of the fundamentalists made many of them hopping mad. Televangelists and church leaders from the fundamentalist camps called Bishop Spong everything from Heathen to Apostate. Spong's deep belief is ,that if Christianity is not rescued from the grip of fundamentalism within the next twenty years, it will cease to have meaning for the majority of Americans. The phenomenon of the European Churches will soon follow through in the United States with fewer than one in ten considering church affiliation as having any relevance or importance.

I would like to quote just one paragraph from Spong to highlight this chapter. "A major function of fundamentalist religion is to bolster deeply insecure and fearful people. This is done by justifying a way of life with all of its defining prejudices. It thereby provides an appropriate and legitimate outlet for one's anger. The authority of an inerrant (literalistic) Bible that can be readily quoted to buttress this point of view becomes an essential ingredient to such a life. When the Bible is challenged, the resulting anger proves the point categorically." (Spong, 1991, p.5)

Spong's point is well taken. Reducing the entire Christian experience to a primitive code where all is perceived as either black or white with no shades of gray creates a comfortable platform from which to judge others. From this comfortable platform the fundamentalists have grown powerful and unchecked. Fundamentalist leaders count on the apathy of the American people for a great deal of their success. Who among us has the time, the ability or the inclination to learn Greek, Hebrew and Aramaic? This general lack of interest and lack of motivation among the masses has fueled much of their platform. There is an old saying which was particularly popular in Nazi Germany. That being, if you say something long enough and with enough conviction, over time it will be accepted as truth.

One aspect of Fundamentalism that is absolutely galling to me is in their desire to pull certain portions of the Old Testament forward, into the New testament in order to make their arguments seem adequate for a church of New Testament believers. On one hand you will hear fundamentalists state that we are washed clean in the blood of the lamb and that the old laws (Laws of Moses) have no bearing over us. This is how one escapes condemnation for eating shell fish, having heterosexual sexual relations during menstruation, wearing garments of dyed material, etc. It is a wonderfully convenient escape from the Laws instituted for the Jews prior to Jesus' earthly ministry and physical resurrection. I would echo my support of this. The laws of Moses were created for the Israelites in order to keep them from diluting their own cultural identity. These Laws have no hold on New Testament believers, AKA Christians. However it is amazing to see how many of these same fundamentalists reach back to Sodom or Leviticus to brush up on their anti-homosexual rhetoric making it of use in today's New Testament church.

I am equally disappointed and dismayed to see a movement within fundamentalism which works to pull additional Old Testament provisions into New Testament life. If they can simply ignore those Old Testament stories and prohibitions which do not directly inconvenience their lives, while pulling forward those which may be used as a sword of judgment on others ,they will increase their power and prestige.

Jude, the latest case of deception

One such area in which rabid fundamentalists are meddling in order to prop up their anti-homosexual rhetoric is in the book of Jude. Before we launch into the book of Jude, I would like to review some basic information regarding the Bible and its construction.

The Eastern Orthodox Church exists today in a pattern of many national churches throughout the world and is most recognized in the United States as the Greek Orthodox Church. In 1054 the churches of the West (Roman Catholic Church) and those of the

East (Eastern Orthodox Church) separated for a great many reasons. One of the hallmark signatures of the Eastern Church has been in its ability to pass on information and tradition in one language, Greek. Those living within the Eastern Church in 1054 would readily recognize the culture and worship of the church as it exists today. This however could not be stated for the Western Church as it has mutated into thousands of denominations with distinctly different orientations.

The New Testament including all of the stories of Jesus' life was written in Greek. The Eastern Orthodox Church was founded in the region closest associated with first century Christianity and its resulting growth. Because the New Testament was written entirely in Greek, in the geographic region of the original writers ,there would logically seem to be no better people to understand or translate its original contents today. The Eastern Orthodox Church maintains a Catechism for its believers in which it offers a brief basis for belief and community life. I would like to quote from *A New-Style Catechism on the Eastern Orthodox Faith for Adults*. "The translation of the original New testament as in the case of any translation is in itself a sort of interpretation and cannot render the full meaning and context of the New Testament." In other words, the Eastern Orthodox Church, the oldest church in Christianity out of which the original language of the New testament came, states that anything but the original Greek version is watered down or changed. The Catechism goes on to explain that the original New Testament was not written down into chapters and verses as we have it today but was one unified work. It wasn't until the creation of the King James Bible, that the books were organized into chapters and verses. The Catechism further states that the division into chapters and verses affords the opportunity for some to use certain verses out of context in order to support a new thought. It went on to say that this is a common mistake which should be avoided. (Mastrantonis, 1969, p.30-31) This seems to support the assertion of the Eastern Orthodox Church which states that any version other than the original is open to flaw, opinion and change.

Watch them pull a rabbit out of their hat
I consider the purposeful misinterpretation of the book of Jude and the new prevailing view of fundamentalism to be a covert, dishonest and disingenuous activity. There is no mention of the sin of Sodom and Gomorrah as having a sexual connotation anywhere throughout the entire New Testament. The fundamentalists have however decided to create a thread from the book of Jude to which they can pull their sexual misconduct (homosexuality) theme of Sodom up from Genesis.

Jude chapter 1 verses 6-7 "And the Angels who did not keep their own domain, but abandoned their proper abode, he has kept in eternal bonds under darkness for the judgment of the great day. Just as Sodom and Gomorrah and the cities around them, since they in the same way indulged in gross immorality and went after strange flesh are exhibited as an example in undergoing the punishment of eternal fire." I would like you to re-read these verses and think about any word or words that may give you a knee-jerk reaction.

Strange flesh is certainly an odd term found within these verses. Strange flesh by today's standard of the English language could have a host of meanings. In order to be faithful to the meaning of any Scripture we must understand the language it was originally written in, the people it was written for and the cultural context in which it was written.

The opportunistic fundamentalists have taken liberty with the words strange flesh changing them to a number of incorrect translations, including unnatural lusts. Unnatural lusts would fit nicely for them as Paul speaks about this in the book of I Corinthians. The reality however is that no biblical scholar in good conscience would ever purposely confuse "strange flesh", translated from the Greek word "SARKS" to have any relation to homosexuality. This however is what the fundamentalists are stating. The "went after strange flesh" at first glance and with no understanding of the word SARKS could easily be confused with their version of the sin of Sodom. This confusion due to the placement and mention of Sodom and Gomorrah is exactly what they are counting on. In addition they are thrilled with versions that have changed the wording to "unnatural lusts" because it drags the true translation one more step toward extinction.

It is often difficult to explain the historical context of a word or concept given today's far removed cultural lenses. During our exploration of Genesis 19 and the Sodom story we were confronted with the fundamentalist view point that the men surrounding Lot's house that night wanted to have sex with the Angels. This in itself is a puzzling concept as most of us have probably never given a thought to celestial beings being sexual in nature.

There are however a number of historical church documents including some Scripture that would lead one to believe that Angels may in fact have been sexual beings. I realize how far-fetched this seems. This is certainly something that no one in Sunday School would have ever uttered. Where did the idea of Angeles being sexual in nature come from? Why hasn't this concept been shared openly with the greater populace? Please keep in mind that any topic dealing with sexuality within the Christian context is often met with displeasure. The concept of 21St century Christianity discussing Angels sexual prowess is beyond most individuals scope of expertise. Although I do not fully support the historical context of Angels having sexual relations I will review its beginnings only because it has a direct relation to Jude Chapter 1.

The Sex lives of Angels

Did Angels ever have sexual relations throughout Scripture and did they ever involve humans? The answer to this question will more than likely surprise you. *Again, I offer this information solely for its relation to Jude 1.* We begin at Genesis Chapter 6, verses 1-4 ; please remember our underlying principal for this study is to determine what the words *strange flesh* or SARKS means, not to determine weather or not Angels are sexual creatures. "Now it came about when men began to multiply on the face of the land and daughters were born to them, that the sons of God saw the daughters of men were beautiful and they took wives for themselves, whomever they chose. Then God said, my spirit shall not strive with man forever because his is also flesh nevertheless his day shall be 120 years." The Scripture goes on to say that Nephleon were on the earth in those days and afterwards when the sons of God came into the daughters of men and they bore children with them. This is pretty simple straight forward stuff. The Sons of God or Angels saw that the daughters of man or Female humans were beautiful and they took whom ever they wanted and bore children, which became the Nephleon, half human, half angel, a race of giants, the mightiest population across all the earth.

The concept of the Nepleon, a race of half human, half Angel beings living upon the earth made an immediate connection to the concept of strange flesh as found in Jude 1. Determined to find further support for this I reviewed as many documents as possible to find other connections. I was led by many published accounts to the term Watchers, which according to Hebrew Theology were Angels sent to earth by God to keep watch over humankind. The Angels from Genesis 6 were in fact these watchers. In order to support this claim I began to discover a multitude of original Hebrew Scripture which was held near and dear to the people of those times which did not make it into the finished canon of the Holy Bible as determined in 393 by the Council of Hippo. I reviewed several versions of the Bible which I have collected over the years to find a reference of the Watchers in relation to Enoch. Enoch is mentioned a number of times throughout the book of Genesis. The book of Enoch was written by the early Hebrews and was considered a part of their canon of authority. The Christian Church however did not include this work among the completed Bible.

Enoch & the Angels
This book of Enoch, older than any New Testament Scripture was written in the old way with no chapters

or verses. I was determined to read the entire work until I found mention of Enoch and the Watchers. Enoch was one of only two people ever who rose to heaven without dying. God desired Enoch's presence so much that he rose to the heavens prior to death. All Hebrew Scripture supports this. Enoch, according to the book bearing his name was an honest, honorable upright man who had a friendship with Angels. He was actually portrayed throughout the book as an advocate for the Angels. Enoch appeared before God's throne in order to defend the Angels who had been upon the face of the earth, pretty much doing whatever they pleased. In a latter edition of the book of Enoch which had the western concept of chapters and verses installed I found Enoch Chapter 1 verse 9 to be God speaking directly to Enoch regarding the Angels activities upon the earth. Enoch 1:9 was word for word verbatim the exact verse as Jude 1:6-7; "And Angels who did not keep their own domain but abandoned their proper abode, he is kept in eternal bonds under great darkness for the judgments of the great day, just as Sodom and Gomorrah and the cities around them, since they in the same way have indulged in gross immorality and went after strange flesh."

The author of the book of Jude was obviously citing Enoch 1:9 in order to bring clarity regarding Hebrew traditions within the new Christian church world. The blending of the Hebrew practice and tradition within the newly emerging Christian church was common. There is no doubt whatsoever that the use of Enoch 1:9 within Jude 1:6-7 was nothing more than the citing of Scripture. For the fundamentalists to purposely mislead those in their care to believe that this verse has anything to do with the sexual immorality of the residents of Sodom is absolute propaganda. The origins of Jude 1:6-7 have been unearthed from mountains of ancient texts. Jude 1:6-7 being used to pull forward a condemnation of Sodom and Gomorrah for sexual perversion (homosexuality) thereby making a clear anti-homosexual statement within the New Testament is absolute and blatant falsehood. Anyone making such a conclusion and preaching it is either ignorant of Biblical exegesis or is a complete and utter liar.

For those of you who may believe that I am only finding what I'd like to find regarding Enoch ,I offer the following in support of my conclusions. The word Pseudepigrapha, refers to the books of the Bible that the church originally used that are not included in the canon today. Until 393 AD the Christian Church used these books and considered them to be a part of their Bible. Just as Jesus quoted Isaiah in the New Testament, the author of Jude quoted from the book of Enoch in Jude 1. The fundamentalists are saying strange flesh, hmmm..., we can couple this odd little statement with the Sodom story and BAM, there you have it, a condemnation of homosexuality within the New Testament. If however an educated public were to produce the story of Enoch, relating its origins to the author of Jude an honest Godly fundamentalist would not be able to refute this, because it is fact.

Genesis Chapter 5, gives us a little background on Enoch because the majority of readers are more than likely unaware of his story. The fifth chapter of Genesis traces the patriarchs before the flood, in other words it traces Adam's lineage. The 18t^h verses states " When Jared was 162 years old he became the Father of Enoch.

After the birth of Enoch, Jared lived for 800 years ...verse 21, When Enoch was 65 years old he became the Father of Methuselah, Enoch walked with God. In all, Enoch lived for 365 years. Enoch walked with God. Then he vanished because God took him." When I quoted the book of Enoch earlier I offered this same information regarding Enoch's life and eventual departure from the earth to be with God. And although the book of Enoch is no longer included within the 66 books of the Protestant Bible this verse in Genesis confirms the information quoted from the book of Enoch. Both the current Bible and the book of Enoch agree that Enoch existed, walked with God and was taken up to heaven without dying. It is my claim that the author of Jude 1 had no intention of tying the sin of Sodom to strange flesh (homosexuality). The verse used in Jude 1 6-7 is a direct quote from the earlier work of Enoch 1:9 and nothing more. If we could find a mention of Enoch within Jude's story it would be crucial in putting any doubt of its origins to rest. Looking further down the page of the letter of Jude we find a most welcome name; Jude 1:14, "It was with them in mind that Enoch, the seventh patriarch from Adam, made his prophecy when he said, "I tell you, the Lord will come with his saints in their tens of thousands, to pronounce judgment on all mankind and to sentence the wicked for all the wicked things they have done, and for all the defiant things said against him by irreligious sinners." Enoch's very name is marvelously preserved within this portion of the book of Jude.

Sodom and Gomorrah had absolutely no connection with strange flesh/ SARKS and cannot be

pulled into the New Testament as a blanket indictment against Homosexual people.

Why was Sodom destroyed?

Why then you may be wondering, after four chapters, was Sodom and Gomorrah destroyed? Ezekiel 16:49 states "Behold this was the guilt of your sister Sodom, she and her daughters had arrogance, abundant food and careless use, but she did not help the poor and the needy." The prophet Ezekiel is stating loud and clear that Sodom was destroyed because of inhospitality. There is also a mention of the sin of idolatry. You will also hear the same message repeated in other Scripture including the book of Wisdom. The book of Wisdom is included in the Catholic, Orthodox and Anglican Bible however it is not included in the 66 books of the Protestant Bible.

The book of Wisdom Chapter 19, verses 13-14 compares the sin of Sodom to Israel's escape from Egypt; "On the sinners, however, punishments rained down not without violent thunder as early warning; and deservedly they suffered for their crimes, since they evinced such bitter hatred toward strangers. Others had refused to welcome unknown men on their arrival, but these had made slaves of guests and benefactors." Hatred towards strangers certainly broke the Rite of hospitality.

The book of Deuteronomy 29:26 "And they went and served other Gods and worshiped them, gods whom they have not known and whom had been no part of their heritage." Again, the concept of worshipping false idols or idolatry is to blame for Sodom's destruction. Again in the Book of Isaiah 3:8-9, the people of Jerusalem are being warned that they better turn from their wicked ways or find themselves in Sodom's shoes, "For Jerusalem has stumbled and Judea has fallen; because their speech and their actions ate against the Lord, to rebel against the glorious presence. The expression of their faces bears witness against them; and they display their sin like Sodom, they do not conceal it. Woe to them for they have brought evil to themselves." They compare Sodom and Jerusalem because they are disobeying by their speech and their actions the laws of God.

Jeremiah 23:14 "Also among the prophets of Jerusalem I have seen a horrible thing, the committing of adultery and walking in falsehood, and they strengthen the hands of evildoers so that no one has turned back from his wickedness. All of them have become to me like Sodom." Walking in falsehood, again refers to idolatry.

Jesus said it, I believe it, that settles it!
Finally Jesus himself makes reference to the destruction of Sodom in Matthew 11:20-24 After Jesus laments the various cities that they have preached to and worked miracles in he instructs his disciples how to go out and spread his message. Verse 24; "nevertheless I say to you that it shall be more tolerable for the land of Sodom in the day of judgment than for you (being those cities who do not accept the disciples)." Jesus is stating that any city that does not receive them or not offer them hospitality will be in more serious trouble than those of Sodom on judgment day. Jesus was comparing Sodom's fate to the act of inhospitality (not receiving his disciples).

5

Boring but essential stuff you must know in order to understand Leviticus

nytime that Gay rights are discussed on a typical American talk show there is always one bright face in the audience waiting to eagerly swoop down quoting Leviticus 18:22 "You should not lie with a man as with a woman, this is an abomination." This quick and easy to commit to memory verse is used and misused constantly against the very existence of Gay persons. This verse offers the greater Christian community the opportunity to overcome prejudice and disconnect hate. This verse is reminiscent of those verses pulled from Scripture fifty to one hundred years ago and used to keep people of color from aspiring beyond second class status. The day of using Leviticus 18:22 as a license to kill ends with the writing of this book. We must however understand the background of this verse, the culture in which it was written and its historical significance. This is absolutely not a one line answer to a one line insult. Study to show thyself approved by God, was first coined to prepare one for such a journey.

The entirety of the Old Testament has to do with the relationship God instituted with humankind. Through all of the misadventures and trials God stood by humankind, always offering the benefit of doubt and the gift of reconciliation. No one group of people has known this more than the Hebrew people. It is through their faith journey that we explore the first half of the Bible. It is through their special relationship with God that we set the blueprint for New Testament Christianity. It is absolutely necessary to understand the journey of the Hebrew people in order to grasp the importance of the book of Leviticus. There are two components that are essential in our understanding of the Leviticus story as it unfolds before us. The components are Covenantal Law, commonly referred to as the Law of Moses and the Babylonian Captivity.

Covenantal Law & the Babylonian captivity
The Covenantal Law or Law of Moses was a series of laws instituted to instill holiness and morality among the Israelites. The Ten Commandments were dwarfed in comparison to the Law of Moses with nearly 700 separate laws or codes of conduct. In order to understand these laws it is important to know how the Old Testament was formed. The first five books of the Bible are known as the Torah, which translated quit literally means the Law. The writing of the Torah was originally attributed to Moses although present day scholars take

issue with the possibility of Moses penning these five books himself. Few take issue with the fact that they were written by close and intimate followers of Moses. There were four major written traditions that were combined to produce a single narrative.

The first tradition is called Deuteronomic. This tradition stresses the need for religious and social reform. Many of the reforms set forth had to do with the removal of idolatry from government branches of power. We will review this tradition much more as we continue this chapter.

The second tradition which shaped the Torah was known as the Priestly tradition. Priestly tradition spoke mostly to the imposition of rules pertaining to religious ritual. They also included the many genealogies proving Gods connection with their people since the beginning of time.

The third tradition from which the Torah was woven is called the Yahwist tradition. This tradition called for political peace and harmony under the established monarchy of Israel. Their accounts were the first known records of Gods relationship to humankind. They emphasized that the God of Israel had saved them as a special people, taking them out of slavery in Egypt.

The fourth and final tradition of the Torah was the Elohist tradition which took special care to explain the covenantal relationship between God and humankind. The Torah achieved its final written form after the Babylonian captivity. These four written styles and traditions were woven together like a fine tapestry so that a single narrative would follow through all of the five books. The untrained eye would never guess that these books were not originally connected and that they had in fact been consolidated at a latter time.

We are going to briefly review the history of how and why the covenantal laws in the book of Leviticus chapters 18 and 20 came into existence. One very important historical event happened outside of the land of Judah about 722 BC. In 722 B.C. Samaria, the royal city of Israel fell to the Assyrians. The Assyrians were a great and powerful military empire who could overwhelm any other land with its military might. The Priestly writers viewed the fall of Samaria, its neighboring land as a fulfillment of Old Testament prophecies. The Priestly writers used this lands fall in order to extol its belief that if a society did not live by the rule of God that it would soon collapse.

During the fall of Samaria many of its inhabitants were displaced, terrified and seeking refuge. Among the refuges were the priests who left their temples in order to survive. The polytheistic Assyrians overturned the priestly laws and implemented their worship of many gods. Their belief of many gods was similar to that of the early Greeks and Romans. The pagan worship that soon ensued in Samaria terrified the nearby neighbors in Judah. Their belief in historical events was a reactive belief system. In other words it was their belief that if a catastrophic event happened to the society up the road they must have done something to deserve it.

The priests who came down from Samaria supported a King by the name of Hezekiah who had decided among many other things that the worship of Baal was wrong and improper. Baal translated actually means worshiping outside of Yahweh (the one God). King Hezekiah decided to strengthen his land by eliminating all worship other than the worship of Yahweh. The priests who had fled Samaria supported the King in his proclamation becoming his biggest promoters. They influenced the King to build one central sanctuary to worship the one God from.

After the completion of this sanctuary the King along with his priestly advisers created a number of moral and religious reform acts...**remember**, if something bad happened to a people they must have brought it upon themselves. The codifying of the moral and reform acts of this time are contained in the book of Leviticus. The book of Leviticus is an extension of the Ten Commandments. The Ten Commandments were apodictic, or straight forward. The latter Covenantal laws were casuistic, arrived at through a process of argumentation and reasoning. The apodictic laws were nonnegotiable while the casuistic laws were arrived at from constant assessment.

King Hezekiah seemed to work wonders during his reign. He established the worship of one God and built a great sanctuary from which to worship. His moral and religious laws contributed greatly to the ordering of their society. It took years for King Hezekiah to get his people on the righteous track and nearly no time at all for his son to reverse everything that he had accomplished.

The book of Second Kings Chapter 21: verses 1-7; "Manasseh was twelve years old when he became King and he reigned for fifty-five years in Jerusalem, his mothers name being Hephzibah. He did evil in the sight of the Lord, according to the abominations of the nations whom the Lord dispossessed before the sons of Israel." As I mentioned earlier, the priestly writers had to give adequate reason for the fall of Kingdoms. "For he rebuilt the high places which Hezekiah his father had destroyed and he erected altars for Baal and had set up a sacred pole as Ahab King of Israel had done and worshiped all of the hosts of heaven and served them all." Hezekiah's son deliberately rolled back all of his fathers reforms, including those relating to the central role of monotheistic religion.

Manasseh put the people back on the track of worshiping false gods. Verses 4-6 continues "And he built altars in the house of the Lord of which the Lord had said in Jerusalem, I will put my name. For he built altars for all the hosts of heaven in the two courts of the house of the Lord, and he made his son pass through the fire, practiced witchcraft and used divination and dealt with mediums and spiritualists. He did much evil in the sight of the Lord, provoking the Lord's anger." Verse seven continues, "Then he set the carved image of Ashura, that he made in a house that the Lord said to David, and his son Solomon, in this house, and in Jerusalem which I have chosen from all tribes of Israel, I will put my name forever." This child-king stripped all of his fathers reforms preferring the worship of false gods and implementing a new society of the old ways. This the priestly writers foreshadow, displeased God greatly. The story of the Hebrew people often portrays them struggling to stay with God, this is the environment in which the book of Leviticus was written.

Although Manasseh put an abrupt halt to his Fathers reforms the struggle for a Monotheistic culture did not end entirely. The prophet Jeremiah 627 B.C. took over where Hezekiah had left off, urging the people and their government to turn back to the righteous ways. Jeremiah pushed for reform through the time of the Babylonian Captivity. We will turn to the book of Jeremiah Chapter 25 in order to understand what the Babylonian Captivity entailed.

The first three verses set the stage for King Nebuchadnezzar, the King of Babylon who desired to add the Israelites to his ever growing population. Jeremiah warns his fellow citizens saying "From the thirteenth year of Josiah the son of Amon, King of Judah, even to this day, these twenty-three years the word of the Lord has come to me." The prophet has warned the people for 23 years that if they did not change that evil would overwhelm them, that the worshiping of false gods would bring disaster to them. In verse 5 he warns "Turn now everyone from this evil way, and from your evil deeds and dwell in the land which God has delivered to you." He continues in verse 6 "And do not go after other gods to serve them and worship them, and do not provoke me to anger with the work of your hands and I will do harm." Jeremiah is foreshadowing the events to come if the people do not turn from their evil ways of worshiping false gods immediately. He points out that the people of Israel were morally and religiously lax, giving themselves as an easy target for political and social take over.

The book of Exodus details how the people of Israel were once held captive by the Egyptians, working as slaves under unjust oppression. Following their exodus the people of Israel, once again free went off to Judah and established their own land. The desire to be both religiously and politically independent was a burning desire of the people as they were once prisoners and slaves. King Nebuchadnezzar and his sprawling

Babylonian empire was well poised for a hostile take-over of the land of Judah. The Babylonian King swept through Judah seizing its land, wealth and religious/political establishments, thus taking the people back into slavery. The prophet Jeremiah like all good priestly writers looks back to his previous warnings and restates many of them again. His belief that if the people were happy living in a society rife with worship of false gods, committing of immoral deeds then their assimilation into the Babylonian culture was a certain outcome.

The tradition and ritual that made the people of Judah special and separate was quickly fading. They were plunged into a melting pot society, losing their ways and incorporating those of the dominant culture.

Two other prophets rose within this time of captivity to give a voice to the people and offer them hope. These were Ezekiel and Isaiah, both claiming that one day God would deliver them from their hopeless captivity. These prophets desired to reignite the will of the people, helping them to rediscover their God and their traditions. The prophets were at least partially correct. The day came when the people were released to repopulate their lost lands. So much time had passed however that many of them had lost their understanding of the uniqueness of their own culture and identity. It was from this period of uncertainty that the priestly writers authored the book of Leviticus. The priestly writers were calling the people back into their own tradition, offering them a guide to achieve this transition.

The completion of the Old Testament which included the Torah and the book of Leviticus is said to have been completed during 70A.D. New Testament readers may wonder how Jesus who was born on 1A.D. could have preached from the Old Testament during his life and ministry if it was not yet completed. Scholars confirm that the 39 books that are now accepted as the Palestinian Bible of the Old Testament (which is used by the Protestant traditions) and the seven additional books known as the Alexandrian Bible (used by Catholic traditions) were actually completed around 70A.D. The reason that this is critical to anyone studying Scripture is to create the understanding that there was plenty of time for updating and revision. Please remember that the Ten Commandments were apodictic or nonnegotiable while the other laws were casuistic or open to revision.

Prior to beginning our study of Leviticus I would like to review the following point. The priestly writers were waging a war for cultural and religious dominance. They believed that the ungodly ways learned prior to and practiced once in Babylon led to their cultural and political downfall. They were all about restoring the old ways.

Reviewing a bit of the history of the people of Israel one can see some early indicators of a coming cultural and religious shift. When the Hebrew people conquered the Canaanite lands and settled there through Abraham they joined a covenantal relationship with God. This was a contract with God, to honor God only, thus becoming the chosen people. The Canaanite people remained in their conquered land and continued their own form of cult worship. The continuation of the Canaanite people in their old ways gave an opportunity for some Hebrew people to view the idol worship, some of which assimilated many of the ideals.

There is an early experience of this mixing the proper Hebrew religion with the Canaanite form of idolatry recorded in Numbers Chapter 25:1-5; "While Israel remained at Shittim the people began to play harlot with the daughters of Moab". Playing the Harlot in Old Testament literature leads back to the concept of worshiping false gods. If one worshiped any God other than the one true God they were a whore. We continue in Numbers "For they invited the people to the sacrifices of their gods and the people ate and bowed to their gods, so Israel joined themselves to Baal and to Peor and the Lord was angry against Israel. And the Lord said to Moses take all of the leaders of the people and execute them in broad daylight before the Lord, so that the fierce anger of the Lord may turn away from Israel." Moses delivered to the leaders the message. They were to slay any of their men who had fallen into the ways of Baal or Peor. This is an early case of the people of Israel taking on some of the cultures of the people with whom they assimilate. God makes it clear within these five verses. It is emphatically forbidden to worship any other gods. The result of doing so is certain death and destruction.

There is one more account of Idol worship that I would like to explore prior to entering Leviticus. Please keep in mind that this is the stage upon which the book of Leviticus enters. Referring to the book of Judges Chapter 10:6-8, Then the sons of Israel, again did evil in the sight of the Lord, served the Baals and the Astora, the gods of Ahriman. The gods of Sideon, the gods of Moab, the gods of the sons of Ammon, the gods of the Philistines. Thus they forsook the Lord and did not serve him. And the anger of the Lord burned against Israel and it sold them into the hands of the Philistines, into the hands of the sons of Ammon.

And they afflicted and crushed the sons of Israel that year. For eighteen years they afflicted all of the sons of Israel who were beyond the Jordan and Gilead in the land of the Amorites." So once again, in the thought process of the priestly writers, if you worshiped any other gods but the One true God severe consequences were sure to follow.

6

Leviticus and the Holiness Codes

Take a deep breath, here goes. Lets begin by turning to Leviticus Chapter 18, verse 22: "Ye shall not lie with a male as one lies with a female, it is an abomination." Several other versions of the Bible have recently changed the word "abomination" to "it is a hateful thing" or "it is a disgusting thing" which bears great importance to our study. The fundamentalists are trying to fuse the knee jerk reaction of typical modern day readers into the Bible verse that is older than almost any other part of the Bible. The word is ABOMINATION, and don't forget it.

The second verse that has offered countless murderers solace as they sit briefly in a cell for killing a Gay person has been Leviticus 20:13 "If there is a man who lies with a male as with a woman; both of them have committed an abomination, they shall surely be put to death their blood guilt is upon them." A number of years ago Vanity Fair magazine published an article titled "Murder in Texas" which followed the stories of young men who delighted in hunting down, torturing and murdering Gay men for sport. Nearly all of those cited in the article could quote this verse from memory and with conviction.

Although these two verses evoke an emotional reaction in many readers I would like to ask you to pause and answer a few simple questions.

Question one: **Who was the book of Leviticus written for?**

Answer: The people of Israel before, during and after their captivity and subsequent release to freedom.

Question two: **Who wrote the book of Leviticus and why?**

Answer: It was written by priestly writers who had fled persecution during the fall of Samaria. It was their belief that if Judah did not turn from worshiping false gods that it too would perish. The book of Leviticus was written for the returning Israelites as *a summary of divine laws to be used in the course of worship.*

I reiterate the above statement. The book of Leviticus was written as a summary of divine law to be applied in the course of worship. The fundamentalist approach of zeroing in on one or two verses within an entire work, pulling only those out that support their presentation and using them totally out of context is morally reprehensible. There will come a time when such religious practitioners will be brought to court for malpractice. Until that time you must be prepared with a ready defense.

The Seventeenth through the Twentieth Chapters of Leviticus are known as the Holiness Code. These codes were enacted in order to keep the cultural purity and religious integrity of the Hebrew people in tact while the pervading social expressions of their time was the act of worshiping idols. I have little patience for our fundamentalist brethren who don't mind throwing rocks at a limited segment of the current population in regards to these two verses yet blindly ignore all the remaining 698.

The Book of Daniel the Third Chapter highlights a little of what life was like for the Israelites during their Babylonian captivity. Verse 1: "Nebuchadnezzer the king made a gold image the height was 60 cubits and the width was 6 cubits, he set it up on the plain of Dura in the province of Babylon. Verse 4: "Then the herald loudly proclaimed, to you the command is given, people and nations, men of every language that at the moment you hear the sound of the horn, the flute...or any musical sound, you will fall down and worship or you shall be immediately cast into the furnace of fire." This well known narrative offers a striking example of what the Israelites faced while in captivity. They would no longer follow their tradions or the ways of their One and only God. Death was certain for those who did not comply to the cultural and religious demands of their captors. They had been cast into a culture in which Kings were revered as gods, under which fertility cults that practiced sexual sacraments abound, under which the Sun, the Moon and all other planets were worshiped. They were a people who had lost their way and worse yet they were forced to culturally assimilate or die. The identity of the chosen people was almost lost.

Jumping back into Leviticus, lets examine the third verse of the eighteenth chapter; "you shall not do what is done in the land of Egypt where you lived, nor are you to do what is done in the land of Canaan where I am bringing you, you shall not walk in their statutes." In other words, God ,through the penning of the priestly writer is reminding the people to stay separate and not to indulge in foreign activities. God is reminding them that they are a select people who must keep their own traditions.

When one reads the prohibitions against male sexual contact which are found in Leviticus without taking them out of context it is very clear to see that the prevalent theme behind them is to prevent the worshiping of idols. Please bear in mind that these people were being assimilated into a culture steeped in fertility gods and that sexually active worship which was acted out within their temples.

It is my contention that if Leviticus 18:22 is pulled out of context its true meaning is corrupted. If we review the twenty-first verse, just above the twenty-second verse we read, "Neither shall you give any offspring, to offer them to Molech, nor shall you profane the name of your God, I am the Lord."

A logical question might be who is Molech? For the non-discriminating fundamentalist the question of "what is being addressed in the verse directly before the verse in question" may never arise. If we are to study in truth with integrity, we must ask this question. Who is Molech and why is this verse directly preceding the prohibition against man laying with man?"

To answer the question who is Molech, we must turn to the book of First Kings the Eleventh Chapter, verses 4-8; "For it came about, when Solomon was old, his wives turned from his heart, away to other gods; and his heart was not wholly devoted to the Lord his God as the heart of David his father had been, for Solomon went after Ashtoreth, goddess of the Zidonians and after Milcom the detestable idol of the Ammonites. And Solomon did what was evil in the sight of the Lord and did not follow fully as David his father had done. Then Solomon built a high place for Chesmosh, the detestable idol of Moab on a mountain which is east of Jerusalem and for **Molech** ,detestable idol of the sons of Ammon. Thus also he did for all of the foreign wives, who burnt incense and sacrificed for their gods."

When one reads the verse "man should not lay with another male" with the realization that the entire book was written as provisions against foreign types of worship, including the sexually charged worship of the countless fertility cults it all comes into focus. When one reviews the verse directly above the "man laying with a man" prohibition and determine that it was a prohibition against Molech, a fertility god, an idol who was worshiped in an open sexual way in public temples, the truth of the Leviticus prohibitions becomes abundantly clear.

Cultic & Temple prostitution

The term within Biblical scholarship "cultic prostitution, or temple prostitution" deals with the worship of fertility gods within the world shared by the Israelites. It is difficult for us to believe, living as we do today that there was once a time in which people would attend a temple service, take a consecrated prostitute from its staff of many and perform sexual acts upon an altar in order to work out ones salvation. It is abundantly clear throughout all of Scripture that this was in fact the case. The fundamentalists normally brush it off when one questions the place of temple prostitution within Scripture but it was a real, venerated, communal religious act in its day.

Earlier we examined the period of time in which the Israelites having left Egypt began to settle in the land of the Canaanites. The world was much different then. There were no church streets with a Presbyterian, Episcopal, Lutheran or Baptist presence. There were however many, many fertility cults who built temples from which to practice their religion. The Hebrew temples were among the smaller communities at this time, they did not have a Cathedral presence. The Cathedral presence however was taken by the fertility cults and their practice of cultic prostitution.

Before examining cultic prostitution I would like to review why I was so absolute back in Leviticus when I said that the verse mistranslated the word ABOMINATION to "a hateful thing, or a wicked thing." The Hebrew language has very deliberate meanings. The word abomination in Hebrew is TOEVAH. Toevah relates directly to the practice of idolatry. Idolatry was considered culturally and religiously wrong, it was "unclean." The word Toevah or "religiously unclean" found its meaning in the temple. When Leviticus was written and the words "man should not lay with another male, it is Toevah" the understanding of this prohibition as fertility cultic religious practice becomes clear. The priestly writers were reviewing what had been witnessed while in the temples during their captivity. (Boswell, 1980, p.100)

Pick out a whore and pray
Scholars have categorized Cultic prostitution or temple

prostitution into three distinct groups. Male prostitution, Female prostitution and Eunuch prostitution. The Eunuch prostitutes had lost their male organs in a desire to become closer to their god as many suspect Roman Catholic priests act out today within celibacy.

Many of the versions of Bibles published today have taken references of temple, cult or sacred prostitutes out and have replaced them with the male "Sodomite" or female "harlot or whore." Please keep in mind that the owners of the publishing companies are mostly fundamentalist folks. They have purposely and with much forethought taken the concept of sacred or temple prostitution out of the Bible in its entirety. In this way current and future Bible readers won't pause and wonder about that funny term, temple prostitute, what? They will however have a deep understanding from an early age that according to their Bible, "the Bible" that sodomites/ homosexuals are sure in for a hard time come judgment day and that their very presence upon the earth is counter to Gods divine plan.

In the book of Deuteronomy the twenty third chapter, verses 17, 18 we read "None of the daughters of Israel shall become cult prostitutes, nor shall any son of Israel become a cult prostitute, you shall not bring the harlot or the wages of the dog into the house of the Lord your God for any votive offering; for both of these are an abomination (TOEVAH) to the Lord." The Imagery of the writers is simple, harlot refers to a female and dog refers to a male. God is saying loud and clear through his priestly writers that bringing a male or temple prostitute into the Hebrew temple and offering them as a sexual sacrifice is toevah, is an abomination. This is not just a striking similarity to "A man laying with a man, this is an abomination", it is the exact reference made in Leviticus. Bringing a female temple prostitute into the Hebrew temple for sexual sacrifice is equally prohibited according to Deuteronomy.

First Kings, Chapter 15, verses 12-13 also deals with temple prostitution. "He also put away the male cult prostitutes from the land and removed all of the idols that his father had made, and he also removed Maachah, his mother from being queen mother because she had made a horrid image as in an Asherah ; Asa cut down her horrid image and burned it at the brook Kidron." Abijam became King of Judah and once again he restored the culture to monotheistic ways. He threw out the temple prostitutes , destroyed the false images and reduced the role of the Monarchy from "god-like" stature to its original human state.

First Kings, Chapter 14:23-24 " For they also built for themselves high places and sacred pillars and sacred poles on every high hill and beneath every luxuriant tree. And there were also male cult prostitutes in the land; they did according to all the abominations of the nations which the Lord disposed before the sons of Israel." Once again the male cult prostitute and idol worship were being used together in the same sentence. It was an epidemic; it was something that they had to deal with in order to keep their own traditions. Could you imagine the reaction of the general public if a temple ,complete with a staff of temple prostitutes, opened next week in any city in this nation? Could you imagine if it opened on church road next to all of the other established churches, synagogues and mosques? One can only imagine that the sanctuary of such a place would see a lot of visitors. This is exactly what occurred. **The established forms of monotheistic worship were losing market share to the countless fertility cult temples**.

And again in Second Kings Chapter 23:5-7, we read, "And he did away with the idolatrous priests whom the King of Judah had appointed to burn incense in the high places in the City of Judah and in the surrounding areas of Jerusalem, also those who burned incense to Baal, to the Sun and the Moon and the constellations and to all the hosts of heaven and he brought out the Asherah (sacred pole) from the house of the Lord outside Jerusalem to the brook of Kidron and burned it, grinding it into dust and throwing its dust on the graves of the common people. **He also broke down the houses of male cult prostitutes which were in the house of the Lord**, where the women were weaving hangings in the Asherah. Second Kings Chapter 23 recalls the great acts of religious restoration brought forward by Josiah who was eight years old when he became King, reigning thirty-one years in Jerusalem. In the twenty-second chapter by way of introducing the religious reforms of Josiah verse two states, "He did what is pleasing to Yahweh, and in every respect followed the example of his ancestor David, not deviating from it to right or left."

The Book of Hosea Chapter 4:14 we read "I will not punish your daughters when they play the harlot or your brides when they have committed adultery for the men themselves go apart with harlots and offer sacrifices with temple prostitutes so the people without understanding are ruined." Hosea is stating that the women of his day should not be prosecuted for sexual misconduct (adultery or temple prostitution) because the men are running to the temples to offer sacrifices with temple prostitutes. In the previous verses of Chapter four, Hosea is indicting the entire country for not acknowledging God in their land. He places a great amount of blame on the priests , denouncing them for not correcting the people, allowing them to "stumble along the way" and calling the priests the "ruin of the people" for their inaction. This verse also points to the fact that both men and women were going to temple, offering sacrifices of a sexual nature on the altars of a false god. The intent of this chapter is simple. It is calling for religious reform and denouncing idol worship. It calls for a return to the true worship of the one God. Several versions of the Bible sum up the end of this chapter differently. The version that I will quote is much older than anything available in the book stores today, the American Standard Bible, published in 1890. It states, "To play the harlot continually, their rulers dearly loved shame, the wind wraps them in its wings and they will be ashamed because of their sacrifices on high altars." This is a simple yet striking image of what Hosea was trying to get across. There were sacrifices on high altars and the lifting up of false gods.

Christian church history supports the validity of temple cult prostitution, which continued well into the Christian era. The church historian Eusebius, the bishop of Caesarea from 260-340 A.D. stated that effeminate priests of the goddess worship at the Mount of Lebanon, engaged in homosexual cult prostitution in his time. We are looking at a publicly supported cultural tradition which began around the time of Moses and continued throughout the first centuries of the Christian Church.

Leviticus 18:22 and 23:13, clearly were not intended as a prohibition against same sex relationships. It is very clear that the authors were speaking about temple prostitution and in relation to idolatry, a very real problem of their time. The struggle of the people of Israel was one in which the supremacy of their one true God must survive. Leviticus was a cultural and religious blue print to ensure the survival of the one true God in the hearts and minds of the Israelites.

7

A New Testament and old tricks Paul faces the reality of temple cult prostitution

Sometime during the several revisions of this manuscript, prior to reaching book form I decided to rename this chapter. The previous name was not very compelling, the Apostle Paul and the book of Romans. It occurred to me during this review process that the fundamentalists waiving Romans Chapter 1:21-32 in defense of their distain for les-bi-gay persons is again an exercise in simple deception. It is the desire of the fundamentalist to take their flawed understanding of Leviticus and pull it forward into the New Testament, thus finding a Christian link to anti-homosexual prejudice and institutionalized hate. Finding that magic bridge that would link the Old Testament hate-talk of "they must surely be put to death" and carrying it forward into the new Christian experience of Jesus would be an absolute bases loaded home run hit. Institutionalized hate of homosexual persons has prevailed in large part due to this flawed desire to unite the misunderstood Old Testament Scripture with the New Testament, which we saw clearly during our study of the book of Jude.

We begin our study of the letter of Paul to the Romans with Chapter 1:21-32, "For even though they knew God they did not honor God or give thanks, but they became futile in their speculations and a foolish heart was darkened. Professing to be wise they became fools and exchanged the glory of the incorruptible God for an image in the form of corruptible man, of birds and four-legged animals and reptiles. That is why God left them to their filthy enjoyments and the practices with which they dishonor their bodies, since they have given up divine truth for a lie and have worshiped and served creatures instead of the creator, who is blessed forever. That is why God has abandoned them to degrading passions, for their women exchange the natural function for that which is unnatural and in the same way also men abandoned the natural function of the woman and burned in their desire towards one another. Men with men committing indecent acts and receiving in their own persons the due penalty of their error. In other words, since they refused to see it was rational to acknowledge God, God has left them to their own irrational ideas and to their monstrous behavior. And so they are steeped in all sorts of depravity, rottenness, greed and malice, and addicted to envy, murder, wrangling, treachery and spite. Libelers, slanderers, enemies of God, rude, arrogant and boastful, enterprising in sin, rebellious to parents, without brains, honor, love or pity. They know what Gods verdict is: that those who behave like this deserve to die and yet they do it; and what is worse, encourage others to do the same."

The Jerusalem Bible which I quoted much of the above from has a bold headline above verses 18 through 32. If you ask Fundamentalists what this headline reads, you will more than likely get a reaction like, "God hates fags", or something slightly less honest. The headlines in bold letters in this Bible reads: **God's anger against the pagans**. The Fundamentalists will purposely begin reading this segment of Scripture beginning at verse 24, "That is why God left them to their filthy enjoyments... Verses 18 through 23 set the stage for the whole meaning of the Scripture. "God's anger against pagans", God's anger against those who once knew him but now enjoin themselves in idol worship and pagan practices.

The Salad bar approach to Bible study

It is typical for the fundamentalist traditions to approach Bible study in a **A+B=C** fashion. As they read bits and pieces of Romans 24-32 they will pick out what they'd like to see; that being, **A**, God gave them up to their unnatural lusts, which they find in verse 24, plus **B**, because men wanted men and women wanted women, that surely equals **C**. **C**, being God gave them over to a depraved mind. I call this the salad bar approach to Bible study. Take only what you wish, while passing by the rest.

Selective Bible study is more closely aligned to political propaganda than it is to discovering truth. In their A+B=C approach they determine that if a homosexual's actions absolved God from caring for them, certainly God's church should have no more concern for them than God himself. This is the clear and simple understanding of the fundamentalist. It is this understanding that has given thousands of them energy to picket the funerals of gay men who died of AIDS. It is through this understanding that they continue to focus on legislation that merely tolerates the presence of lesbians and gays in society as long as they are held in check. It is through this understanding that thousands of gay and lesbian people have departed this world estranged from their families, their friends and their religion. A+B=C is simple, it is quick and it requires very little soul searching or thought. A Black and White approach to life insures that those pesky Grays don't keep one awake at night, as one struggles with the unknown or the not too certain. Faith is never an issue of black and white and is almost always an issue of gray. Jesus' love, Jesus' example and Jesus' call for us to witness has never been simple and has never been easy. Fundamentalism equals easy and quick solutions, no pondering, easy answers, black and white, no gray.

The Fundamentalists will read Romans Chapter One, as if it was a newspaper story, as if they walked right up to a vending machine, dropped in a quarter and pulled out a copy of USA today, the front page reading, **"Men sleeping with Men, Women with women, God gave them up to a depraved mind."** They will take this translation, which has much to do with the social times and the significance of history in the first century of the church in Rome or Corinth, including the influence of pagan religions during that time and honestly read it as if it were hot off the press. Fundamentalists have a way of mentally processing

Scripture as if it were written today in our context and culture, choosing not be bothered by all of the details. It is only when one studies the events , customs, languages and times of 54 A.D. that light can be shed on the entirety of the Scriptures meaning.

Words are always in motion

I would like to demonstrate just how difficult it can be to understand something in its entirety, written during a different point in time. I will offer an example in English which is certainly much easier for any of us to consider than Greek or Hebrew. The example, taken from an Anglican publication begins by stating that words are like little children, they are always in motion, for example, "Back in 1675 just nine years after the terrible London fire had devastated so much of the city, Sir Christopher Wren laid the cornerstone of what was to be the most ambitious undertaking, the rebuilding of Saint Paul's Cathedral. He worked on the project for over 35 years and the experts said that he pored more of his genius into this edifice then to any other building he had ever designed. When the project was finally completed and Sir Christopher himself was a very old man, he personally conducted the then reigning monarch, Queen Anne on an extensive tour through the whole building. When the tour was over he waited with baited breath for her reaction. In typical British terseness she used three adjectives to sum up her feelings: "It is awful, it is artificial, and it is amusing." Can you imagine how the old builder must have felt when the one person's opinion whom he valued the most described his Magnum Opus in this way? We are told that Sir Christopher let out an audible sigh of relief, sank to his knees and thanked her Majesty for her graciousness."

When I first read this, I thought that Sir Christopher must have either gone deaf in his old age or that he suffered an immediate nervous breakdown, causing his reaction to the Queen's appraisal. Words are always in motion and never stand still. If you look back to this era, the word **awful** meant **awesome or awe inspiring.** The word **artificial** meant **artistic.** The word **amusing** meant **amazing.** Words are ever changing, social order is ever changing, traditions and customs are ever changing and this story highlights how a language as familiar as English could possibly 400 years later be totally misunderstood by a civilization that also speaks, reads and writes in English.

The realty of Romans Chapter One was that Paul's fledgling community was in constant competition for souls with the better organized, more entrenched pagan religions of his day. The Scripture is obviously speaking of former believers who have "given up the glory of the immortal God for a worthless imitation" **idol worship**, in the form of "corruptible man, birds, four legged animals and reptiles." The references to same sex activities are obviously a reference to **temple cult prostitution**, which is historical fact. Justifying Romans Chapter One as God's distain for Homosexuals is in many ways similar to how those who were opposed to abolitionism justified slavery, the separation of the races, institutionalized bigotry and hate based on race and ethnicity. Although embarassing to many church leaders portions of Scripture have been used to oppress or repress people based on a perception of minority status.

The Gibeon deception

While Romans Chapter One is still fresh in your mind, it would be a good time to review Joshua Chapter 9:3-27. This story opens with the inhabitants of Gibeon, well informed of Joshua's great military success in taking down Jericho. The Gibeonits are in fact nearby neighbors of the Israelites, living in the land of the Canaanites. Fearing hostile military attack from Joshua they set out to trick the people of Israel. Please remember how Joshua and his forces treated the people and livestock of Jericho. The Gibeonits determined to survive with as little loss of life as possible undertook a plan by which they would appear to be distant, uninformed travelers. They dirtied their clothes and strapped on their oldest, most worn out shoes in order to be viewed as people who had traveled a long and hard journey. They also packed stale foods , old dried out bread which would normally be thrown away, only people who had traveled far would have stale food. Then they formed a long straight line and marched right into the land of the Israelites. As they came upon the area in which the Israelites had settled, they counted on a few things. They counted on the fact that the Israelites were a people of their word, knowing that they were a people who established covenants. They also counted on the fact that once a covenant was set in place, they would be spared the same outcome as the people of Jericho. The Gibeonites were correct in all of their strategies. They were treated as travelers rather than enemy combatants.

It is not until verse 20 that someone catches on, realizing that they have been duped. "This we will do to them, even let them live, lest wrath be upon us for the oath which we swore to them." In other words, it's too late to kill them, we've already signed a contract, although no one could argue it was under false pretenses. Fine then, we simply won't kill them. Verse 21 states "And the leaders said to them, Let them live so that they be hewers of wood and drawers of water for the whole congregation, just as the leaders said, the community did." Let them be woodcutters and water carriers for the whole of the Israelite community.

Let's take this story and break it down into a simple Fundamentalist A+B=C format.

A=the inhabitants of Gibeon purposely set out to fool the Israelites into signing a peace agreement or covenant. B=the Israelites believed the deception and supported the covenant of irrevocable peace between them and the Gibeonites. And C= the people of Gibeon, those people who had deceived the Israelites upon being realized would be put into slavery.

Romans 1, a new wrinkle to an old process

I have been told of editions of the Bible up to one hundred and forty years ago that actually inserted the words Let them live, *"they will turn black"*... into the twenty-first verse in order to support institutionalized slavery. Most of these editions disappeared through embarrassment, long before most reading this were born. During the Civil War most of the churches of the North supported the freedom of all human beings, including those who had been forced into slavery. In the South most churches of the same denominations as those in the North, supported their right to slavery by citing Joshua chapter Nine as being part of God's divine plan. They were the people who proclaimed,

"Who can challenge the mind of God in such things?" People of the same mind set today use Romans Chapter One in the same manner as their ancestors used Joshua Chapter Nine.

When one compares the prohibitions of Leviticus to Romans Chapter One it is apparent that the author of Romans, the Apostle Paul was repeating the warning of Leviticus in relation to temple prostitution and idol worship to his new believers. Unlike Paul, many of them had never studied the Hebrew Scriptures. The question of Leviticus being repeated in Romans comes down to the person who wrote Romans, Paul himself. Paul introduces himself very well in Acts 22:3, "I am a Jew, and I was born at Tarsus in Cilicia. I was brought up here in this city. I studied under Gamaliel and was taught the exact observance of the Law of our ancestors." In Paul's own words, he is a Jew, who was brought up strictly observing (*exact observance*) the law of Moses.

There are two verses attributed to Paul's writings which the fundamentalists believe support their bias against Gay, Lesbian and Bisexual people. They are Romans 1:24-26, and I Corinthians 6:9 .

Paul was a Jew of a Roman province, educated by one of the most scholarly Rabbinical minds of his day, Gamaliel. Gamaliel was to the first century Judaism what the Dali Lama is to Tibetan Buddhism today. People traveled thousands of miles just to sit at his feet.

Paul's resume.
In Acts 22:20 Paul states that he actually took part in and witnessed the murder of St. Stephan, the first accepted martyr of the Christian faith. St. Stephan was murdered because he disliked the walls being raised

around his new faith. He tired of the involvement of those who wanted Christianity to mirror the Jewish tradition in its upholding of the law. St. Stephan was murdered much like Jesus, he was put in front of a tribunal who was determined to kill him and instead of crucifying him, they pummeled him to death.

Paul, the devoted believer in the law and all things traditional actually took part in the killing of Stephen. In Acts Chapter Nine we find the conversion of Paul on his way to destroy other Christians lives in a nearby city. The blinding light of God leaves him completely unable to see, lying in the road. The voice of God is audible from the blinding light and asks, "Saul (Hebrew form of Paul) why are you persecuting me?" God speaks directly to Paul on the road to Damascus, convincing him to convert to Christianity and follow Jesus. This ends his life's earlier chapter of Christian-bashing by Paul. He becomes a zealous winner of souls for Christ, much as he had been a zealous keeper of the law.

Paul was able to incorporate his belief of the old ways into his new faith experience. In Acts Chapter 19:26 we see Paul continuing to turn people away from idol worship and toward the one true God. "nearly everywhere in Asia ,Paul has persuaded and converted a great number of people with his argument that gods made by hand are not gods at all." This was Paul's message throughout the writing of the New Testament, that gods made by hand are not gods at all.

8

God's made by hand are not gods at all

I have noted, that when the going gets tough, the fundamentalists whip out good ole I Corinthians 6:9. This one verse, particularly as it has been re-translated in the Bibles printed after the late 1970's has been responsible for more attacks on Gay, Lesbian and Bisexual persons than any other in the New Testament. The mis-use of this one verse has led thousands of Lesbigay persons to turn from their churches, their families and in many instances their faith. I take great pleasure in offering a different opinion on Paul's letter to the Corinthians. Although the Bible as we know it today groups Paul's letters in numerical order, First Corinthians, followed by Second Corinthians it is thought that it may not have originally been the case. Scholars believe that Paul wrote a total of four letters to the early church of Corinth and that the first one did not survive. The earliest portions of this existing letter was written while Paul resided in Ephesus around 57

A.D. Paul visited the church of Corinth to assist them in assimilating into the new Christian faith experience and to quell discontent. Later Paul decided to send an emissary in his place with another letter. Neither the emissary nor his message was received by the people of the church. A third letter known as a "severe letter" was then penned because the people of the church in Corinth seemed absolutely unmanageable. Paul was obviously reacting to some pretty intense issues. This third letter seems to have set much of the blue print for what Paul considered proper Christian living.

The Jerusalem Bible which I have referenced several times prior has a good background statement relating to Paul's letters. Regarding the letter to the church of Corinth it states "Corinth, a great and populous port, was a magnet to every sort of philosophy and religion and was also a notorious center of immorality. Paul's converts in the city were particularly in need of instruction and guidance, both about the Good News itself and about Christian life which it implied. The two letters to the Corinthians contain much information about urgent problems that faced the church and the important decisions which were made to meet them: questions of morality, about liturgy, the holding of assemblies, the recognition of spiritual gifts and the avoidance of contamination from pagan religions" (Jerusalem Bible p. 195)

A Moral Decadence sandwich

The portion of Paul's First letter to the Corinthians which I Corinthians 6:9 is found is literally sandwiched between two discussions of moral decadence. Paul is convinced that the people within the church are being influenced by their society and culture. In the Fifth chapter of I Corinthians, Paul takes on a church member who is practicing incest. Paul writes "This is a case of sexual immorality among you that must be unparalleled even among pagans." Paul continues by saying that a person living in this manner openly should have been expelled from the church community. Paul concluded this chapter by stating that it is not his business to pass judgment on those within the Corinthian society who live outside of the church. If believers followed this Pauline request literally it would be a refreshing improvement to Fundamentalist Christianity. In Chapter Six however Paul takes issue with church members who still feel compelled to take their moral vesting from the courts of the city. Paul starts in a stern tone "How dare one of your members take up a complaint against another in the law courts of the unjust instead of before the saints?" In other words Paul was saying that the church members should live separately from their secular peers and that if an issue arose among them that it is through the churches tribunal that justice would be served. Paul continues by reminding the members of the church that if they are to survive as a community it will be through trust and consideration of one another rather than through wronging and cheating one another. Verse Nine picks up after all that I have outlined above and today reads in most Bibles, "For do you not know that the unrighteous shall not inherit the Kingdom of God, do not be deceived, neither fornicators, nor idolaters, nor adulterers, nor effeminate, nor homosexuals, not thieves, nor the covetous, nor drunkards, nor revilers, nor swindlers shall inherit the Kingdom of God."

The second half of the sandwich of which I mentioned earlier follows in verse 12 through 20 and is actually separated from the verses above. Paul apparently was once quoted as saying "For me there are no forbidden things", speaking out of the conviction that Christians were no longer slaves to the Laws of Moses. This statement was apparently picked up by others within the church who used the saying creatively in order to excuse immoral behaviors. This portion of the letter was directed to a group known as the Libertines who taught that sexual intercourse was as necessary for proper health as was food and drink. Paul continues his comments by stating that food is for the body but the body was not made for fornication. "To fornicate is to sin against your body." Chapter Seven continues by outlining the virtues of marriage and virginity.

It is obvious from the historical elements pulled together within the text of I Corinthians that Paul was reasserting some sense of control over a membership who seemed to fall back into old habits. It would be from Paul's strong Rabbinical training that he would outline his views of morality, mostly as noted in the book of Leviticus. Although Paul knew that they were no longer slaves to the law, he concluded that some rules of conduct must be established especially in wild port cities like Corinth. The members of Paul's community were Hellenic Jews, Jews of Greek origin. They established a few small community churches in the synagogues. Paul brought these former believers of the law into a life of reconciliation through Christ. He had to however reinforce constantly that reconciliation without repentance was like slapping a gift giver in the face after being offered a gift. Corinth was a great port city of the Roman Empire, it was located in Greece on a narrow strip of land that connected the north and south and it was the shortest trade route between Europe and Asia. Corinth was a vital seaport for both travel and shipping. As in the case with many great seaport cities, Corinth attracted diversity. Diverse people, diverse religion and broad social norms. If Corinth existed today as it once did, I would imagine it would be a lot like San Francisco.

History tells us that among the diverse religious institutions present in Corinth that none was more awe inspiring or as outrageous as the Temple of Aphrodite. Aphrodite was of course, the Greek goddess of fertility cults and her temple was known throughout the world for employing a staff of 1000 sacred temple prostitutes. We discussed the office of temple prostitutes throughout our study of the Old Testament Scriptures. Aphrodite and her mega-temple in Corinth offers much insight to Paul's letter to the Corinthian church members. To the south of the seaport city was Acrocorinth, the mountaintop site of several pagan temples. Apollo had a temple, Athena had a temple, Poseidon even had a temple there. (Day, 1987, p.107)

In Paul's letter to the Corinthians he refers to the city of Corinth by stating that "there are gods and lords aplenty". Now you'll remember that when we traced Paul's background he went from a Christian-killer to being a Super-Christian. One important issue from his past religious practice hitched a ride into his new expression, that being a contempt for any religion outside of the worship of the One, true God. Paul clearly restates this almost in a fanciful way in I Corinthians

8:5 by saying Corinth is a crazy place, it has gods and lords aplenty, no shortage of odd deities.

Corinth was widely regarded as a city of pleasure and a city of vice. The cities reputation forced its way into the Greek language by joining the name of the city with the concept of prostitution in the words Korinthia Kore, which loosely translated means Corinthian female prostitute and Korinthiastes, meaning businessman or even more loosely translated as whore-monger. Another word, Korinthtazesthat loosely translated means "to play the Corinthian" or to visit a house of prostitution. (Day, 1987, p.108)

The god Apollo's temple was nearly as impressive as the Temple of Aphrodite. Aphrodite was after all the goddess dedicated to female beauty and Apollo was the god dedicated to male beauty. Those joining in worship within these temples would be brought to a frenzy during the course of the service leading to sexual expression. The sexual relations practiced within these temples included all dynamics of human sexuality, including heterosexual and homosexual relations. It is mind boggling but true that all of this took place during the ritual of worship, on the altar and throughout the temple area.

Paul was at war with these polytheists and their ritual uncleanliness. His firm foundation within Judaism gave him a strong desire to stomp out any worship other than that of the One, true, God. He took his mission of spreading the word of life in Christ very seriously. The responsibility of holding this new church together in a time in which anyone could go to a temple and select one of a thousand or more temple prostitutes to act out with must have been maddening. The church that Paul was planting was considered to be the fringe-element and the established temples of cultic prostitution were the established norm of the society.

It is understandable that Paul desired to insulate his new followers from the outside forces of secular living of their day. It is however difficult for me to believe that many of Paul's followers living today continue in this practice. With this thought in mind and with the full knowledge of who is buying up the rights to modern Bibles and why, I turned to a stack of Bibles in my study to do a small sampling of how the revisionists within fundamentalism are turning back the progressive clock of Christianity. The Bible of favor within the fundamentalist circles is the New American Standard Bible which translates 1 Corinthians 6:9 as "Nor idolaters, nor adulterers, nor effeminate, nor homosexuals..." The New International version which was originally penned in 1973 then updated in 1984 is similar "Nor idolaters, nor adulterers, nor male prostitutes, nor homosexual offenders..." The word homosexual deliberately stamps out the correct translation of "effeminate" as male prostitutes. Looking back to the good old King James version we read "Nor idolaters, nor adulterers, nor effeminate, nor abusers of themselves with mankind..." The New King James written in 1984 states, "Nor idolaters, nor adulterers, nor homosexuals, nor sodomites..." however it does include an asterisk and at the bottom of the page where we find this word, *catamites. I continued my survey turning to the American Standard published in 1885 "Nor idolaters, nor adulterers, nor effeminate, nor abusers of themselves with men..." I also checked the New Jerusalem Bible finding..."idolaters, adulterers, the self-indulgent and sodomites..." In this version the word homosexuals was replaced with the words, "self-indulgent". I originally found this to be puzzling. My favorite version of Scripture, the original Jerusalem Bible of 1966 states "Idolaters, adulterers, catamites and sodomites…" And finally I turned to the New Revised Standard Bible to find, "Idolaters, adulterers, male prostitutes, sodomites…"

It is unimaginable that Paul's writings reflected anything close to what we understand today as homosexuality. Paul's prohibitions were against ritual and cultural uncleanliness not about living in a loving relationship. The term Homosexual which the fundamentalists mindlessly interject wasn't even born until the late 1800's by German physicians. Again, turning to the original source of an original language seems to be the best process in this search for truth. The Greek New Testament uses neither homosexual, nor abusers of themselves with mankind. It does however use the work "Malakoi". The second word appearing in this verse is "Arsenokoitai". The Greek translation most cited for the word malakoi is "voluptuous person." In trying to understand the cultural connotation associated with the word malakoi, I search the remainder of Scripture for other uses. I found them in some rather odd places.

Matthew's Gospel uses the word malakoi in the eleventh chapter verses 7 & 8; "And as these were going away, Jesus began to speak to the multitudes about John, "What did you go out into the wilderness to look at?" they asked, he answers saying "A man dressed in Malakoi, a man dressed in soft clothing. This would lead one to believe that Malakoi translated literally means soft clothing. Luke tells the same story in his

Gospel, chapter seven verses 24 & 25, "But what did you go out to see, a man dressed in soft clothing? Behold those who are splendidly clothed and live in luxury are found in Royal palaces." This supports Matthews use of the word. In both cases when the word Malokoi left the tongue of Jesus Christ it meant **soft**.

Scholars tend to believe that Malokoi was a cultural put-down, reserved for those in society not fitting the norm. The most general definition evoked by scholars is that the meaning refers to a weakness in moral character. If it was in fact used as a cultural put-down, one might refer to the lazy as malokoi, to drunks as malokoi, to someone too pristine for the norm as malokoi, you could use it broadly and across the board, however it has no direct relation to homosexuality as it is known today. Jesus certainly wasn't talking about a man in homosexual clothing in the Gospel.

It appears that "soft" was replaced in the Seventeenth century with the word effeminate. When we checked the literal meaning of malokoi in Greek we found voluptuous person. This was certainly not the meaning used by the English, translating voluptuous into effeminate as we know it today, makes no sense. The word effeminate used by the English at this time translated directly to "Self-indulgent" and Self-indulgent meant voluptuous.

St. John Chrysostom was one of the early church fathers responsible for a great deal of Christian doctrine. St. John had a real problem with homosexuality in his day. He made no bones about it, he didn't like monks sneaking into one another's bunks late at night and he wrote extensively about sex outside of wedlock. The most interesting fact regarding St. John Chrysostom, the Jerry Fawell of his day, is that he personally wrote extensively about Paul's letters, never even once making a connection regarding "the abuses" of the early church with homosexuality. This man detested homosexual behavior, yet he never made a connection between it and Paul's writings. Now if St. John Chrysostom, who was A., a great disliker of homosexual behavior and B., a speaker, reader and writer of ancient Greek, never drew the conclusions of today's Fundamentalists, one must wonder what conclusions St. John made. St. John, upon whose teachings still hang the Greek Orthodox's prohibition of homosexuality today, wrote that St. Paul's use of Malokoi meant "**those who "Masturbate"**". Those soft, self indulgent, non-procreating masturbators.

The very ancient Greek writings of church law and Christian morality appear together today within a 1084 page book of canons known by English speakers as "the Rudder." St. John Chrysostom and the other early church Fathers agreed that Paul was in fact speaking out against the immoral practice of masturbation, in their summation of Paul's text on page 937 they state that First Corinthians 6:9 referred to "Masturbation not only causes the soul damage everlasting, but also causes damage to the health of the body, the soul is caused damage everlasting and the body and the soul are deprived of the Kingdom of Heaven, as it is condemned to perpetual punishment in hell, as St. Paul states, "Be not deceived, neither fornicators, neither idolaters, nor adulterers, nor masturbators, nor those guilty of sodomy shall inherit the Kingdom of God." (Rudder, 1957, p.937) The Ancient laws of Christian conduct written in ancient Greek by the early church Fathers agree that Malokoi has nothing to do with homosexual persons.

The ancient Greek translation of Malokoi, meaning soft, stood within the church and was translated as "those who masturbate." The question as to why a word meaning masturbators would ever be changed to homosexuals must be asked. The answer is quite simple. In light of the broadened understanding of human sexuality great minds, many of which were Christian came to understand that masturbation was not evil or deserving of eternal damnation, just a simple process of human sexuality. A decoy or a scapegoat was needed however as Scripture doesn't just fade away. If the majority of society masturbate, therefore are hell-bound, perhaps there is a way to minimize the damnation aspect of the verse. The way to minimize the damnation aspect was simply to redirect the damnation away from the majority and onto a minority. With the church pews still ninety percent filled few ever noticed the ten percent who no longer attended. Masturbators were in and homosexuals were out.

9

Who needs this book?

The surest answer to this question is everyone who is either Gay, Lesbian, Bisexual and/or anyone who cares for any Lesbigay persons, friends, relatives and/or anyone who believes in the concept of fairness and embraces it without concern for the opinion of the misinformed. You may say, "I'm not even Christian, so this has nothing to do with me." My answer to this is that those who proclaim to be Christian, who pervert the meaning of Scripture for their own advantage may use their understanding to impact your life regardless of your own faith expression or lack thereof. A humorous bumper sticker that I have enjoyed greatly makes this point quite well. The words JESUS SAVE ME appear in bold letters followed by the smaller words "from your followers." This is a very powerful message for any who have been disenfranchised. It is not Jesus who evokes fear in the hearts and minds of persons living on societies margins, but his poorly educated followers who blindly claim to continue his works on earth today.

In 1993 the National Academy of Science, published a landmark book entitled, "The Social impact of AIDS in the United States." This study saw fit to invest forty of two hundred and ninety five pages on the topic of religion and religious groups. Page 132 offers what I consider a stunning statement on the place of fundamentalist Christians during the first decade of the AIDS pandemic. "The Christian right sees such people as secular humanists, abortionists and homosexuals, not only as deviants by their activities but being major causes of the breakdown of America's moral standards. Thus homosexuals by association, persons living with AIDS may serve as scapegoats for conservative fundamentalists so that they might blame someone for the moral decay that they see all around them. This suggestion is given further empirical support by a series of studies showing that hostile attitudes toward gay men and lesbians are consistently and positively correlated with certain religious behaviors and attitudes, such as literal belief in the Bible and frequency of church attendance." (Jonsen, Stryker, 1993 p.131, 132)

The preceding paragraph illustrates just how powerful conservative fundamentalists are now finding themselves in the United States and why this book and its message of inclusivity is important for all, not only those sexual minorities directly effected by the strength of the far right. The United States Government reached this conclusion given the above paragraph. It is rare to find such clarity in a governmental publication or report.

This same un-Christ like mentality led fundamentalist icon Jerry Falwell to preach a message of shame and intolerance toward gays in a sermon entitled "How many roads to heaven?" delivered on national television. In this now infamous sermon, Falwell stated, "God was bringing an end to the sexual revolution through the AIDS epidemic." He also stated that "They, (i.e., gays), were scared to walk near each other and that what preachers have been unable to do for hundreds of years, in preaching, a God who hates sin has stopped dead in its tracks by saying, "Do it and die, do it, and die." Falwell's political organization, the Moral majority, parent organization to the Christian coalition, opposed governmentally researched AIDS projects of all kinds because the disease was a gay problem. Such statements were printed throughout the pages of Christianity Today and from US News and world report (1985). Falwell promoted the idea that "AIDS was not only God's judgment on gay men, but also that divine judgment extended to all of society. AIDS is a lethal judgment of God in America for endorsing this vulgar perverted and reprobate lifestyle." (Jonsen, Stryker, 1993, p.131-132)

Please also remember that on September 12, 2001 it was evangelical fundamentalist preacher Jerry Falwell that blamed the terrorist attacks in New York City on gays, abortionists and feminists. Falwell didn't miss the opportunity of pinning something as despicable and horrifying as the murder of thousands of innocent citizens to the sleeve of Gay and Lesbian persons, just as Hitler and the SS pinned pink triangles to their prison sleeves.

The organization known as PFLAG, Parents and Friends of Lesbians and Gays, has connected dramatically with the issue of marginalization. PFLAG holds support group meetings for the parents and friends of

Lesbigay persons who are trying to come to terms with their loved ones sexuality. Among many great works within their publication society, is a very passionate one page tract that was published by PFLAG many years ago, telling the personal life experience of Mary A. Griffith in her own words. I will paraphrase somewhat without losing the power of the message.

"Because of my lack of knowledge, I became dependent upon people in clergy, when the clergy condemns a homosexual person to hell and eternal damnation, we the congregation echo, Amen! When the clergy says a homosexual person is sick, perverted and dangerous towards children, we again echo, Amen! I deeply regret my lack of knowledge concerning gay and lesbian people, had I allowed myself to investigate, what I now see as Bible bigotry and diabolical dehumanizing slander against our fellow human beings, I would not be looking back with regret for having relinquished my ability to think and reason with other people, people I trust for truth and guidance in my life and the life of our gay son, God did not heal or cure Bobby, as he, our family and clergy, believed he should be. It is obvious now why he did not. God has never been encumbered by the children's genetically determined sexual orientation. God is pleased that Bobby was a kind and loving heart. In God's eyes, kindness and love are what life is about. I did not know that each time I echoed , Amen to the eternal damnation, referring to Bobby as sick, perverted and a danger to our children, that his self-esteem and personal worth were being destroyed.

Finally, his spirit broke beyond repair, he could no longer rise above the injustice of it all. Bobby ended his own life at age twenty. It is not God's will that Bobby jumped over the side of a freeway overpass into the path of an eighteen wheel truck, killing him instantly. Bobby's death was the direct result of his parent's ignorance and the fear of the word "Gay", an injustice has been done not only to Bobby, but to his family as well, God knows it is not right that Bobby is not here with his loved ones. Correct education about homosexuality would have prevented this tragedy. There are no words to express the pain and the emptiness remaining in our hearts for Bobby and his family members, relatives and friends. We miss Bobby's kind and gentle ways, his fun-loving spirit and his laughter. Bobby's hopes and dreams should not have been taken from him, but they were. We can't have Bobby back, if we could we would say to him, as I say to all gay and lesbian people around the world, those benevolent words of Leo Buscalia, "Love yourself, accept yourself, forgive yourself and be good to yourself, because without you the rest of us are without a source of wonderful things." There are children like Bobby sitting in our congregations, unknown to you. They are listening to your Amen's, as they sit silently they cry out to God in their hearts, their cries will go unnoticed for they cannot be heard above your Amen's. Your fear and ignorance of the word gay will soon silence their cries. Before you echo, Amen, in your home or in your place of worship, think and remember a child is listening." Mary Griffith has eloquently encapsulated the essence of this books mission and I sincerely thank her for it.

In 1989, while George Bush, senior, was President of the United States, a study by the U.S. Department of Health and Human Services concluded that suicide among young people, confused over their sexual orientation was a leading cause of death in teenagers through out the United States of America. The study although suppressed for some time was eventually released with much feet dragging by the administration. This and several studies since have stated the following facts:

- Young Gays and Lesbians are 6 times more likely to attempt suicide than their heterosexual peers.
- As many as twenty-three percent of Lesbian and Gay men attempt suicide.
- Gay and Lesbian youth have been projected to comprise thirty percent of those suicides completed annually.
- If a Gay or Lesbian adolescent or young adult attempts suicide and initially fails, there is a far greater probability that they will attempt suicide again.

These are striking facts supported by credible research. A civilized society would be ashamed of these statistics. (Counseling Issues with Gay & Lesbian adolescents, 3 June 2005)

Not long ago while presenting to a class at a liberal University in California, I found a poster tacked to the wall among several others. This was not a college job announcement or a roommate request. The nature of the poster was far more insidious. The opening statement of this poster read "Do you or a loved one need help?" This opening question was followed up with the hook, "Please call homosexuals anonymous for the nearest Christian reparative therapy clinic." The poster gave no notice to the passers-by that the American Psychiatric Association has considered reparative therapy to be unethical at best and criminal at worst. The opening phrases give way to a laundry list of nazi-style assaults on one segment of society. "Facts about homosexuality: Homosexuals spread disease. Homosexuals comprise one percent of the population but account for half of all syphilis cases. Three fourths of all homosexuals have had Hepatitis B. Ninety percent demonstrate chronic, viral infections with the Herpes virus. Currently there are about 250 million citizens in the United States, which means that there are roughly 2.5 million homosexuals. There are also 1 million people with the AIDS virus, 80% of them homosexuals. That means there are 800,000 sodomites carrying the HIV virus. 2.5 million homosexuals in the U.S. divided by 800,000 HIV positive sodomites means that 1 of every 3 homosexuals are spreading the AIDS virus. Homosexuals are sexual deviants. The average male has 7.3 sexual partners in his life. The average homosexual has over 100 sexual partners per year and one quarter have over 1,000 partners thus far in life. Even though sodomites are only 1% of the population they account for 30% of all child molestation cases and three-fourths of all homosexuals have had sex with children under the age of 16. Homosexuals are violent, they are 15 times more likely to commit murder than non-homosexuals." As if the above statements of false-facts are not damaging enough to the potential reader, the hook ,soon follows. "Homosexuals can be cured. God can overcome any adversity even homosexuality. Faith in Jesus Christ has led thousands of people out of the bondage of homosexuality. If you'd like help to be cured of homosexuality, please call."

This poster, tacked among other college-life materials illustrates just how much further this society needs to stretch in order to understand its biased outdated assumptions are nothing more than lies told and retold.

It was Hitler's minister of propaganda who said that if one tells a lie over and over again with enough conviction, soon it will become truth. Posters very similar to this were once posted in all Nazi occupied territories. If the word "homosexuals" is replaced in most of these statements with "Jews," a stunning replica of Nazi propaganda materials emerge.

It will take more than a few interested Lesbigay individuals to ensure that the oven's of societal oppression do not fire up again, marking a new season of execution. It will take all of the good people living in both the Blue and Red States across the United States and abroad. If challenges are not made based on factual information, life experience and fairness, we will be cursed as a people to repeat the folly of the past. It is my prayer that this book will in some small way bring us all closer together as a people and ultimately closer to the God who created us.

We believe in one God, the Father, the Almighty, maker of heaven and earth, of all that is, seen and unseen... The Nicene Creed

"In the beginning was the Word, and the Word was with God, and the Word was God. He was in the beginning with God. All things came into being by Him, and apart from Him nothing came into being that has come into being." The Gospel of John, 1:1-3

Works Cited

Boswell, John. *Christianity, Social Tolerance, and Homosexuality.* Chicago, IL: The University of Chicago Press, 1980.

"Counseling Issues with Gay and Lesbian Adolescents." 3 June. 2005 www.youth.org/loco/PERSONProject/Resources/OrganizingResources/counseling.html.

Day, David. *Things They Never Told You in Sunday School.* Norwalk, CT: The Lavender Press, 1987.

Jones, Alexander, Editor. *The Jerusalem Bible.* Garden City, NJ: Doubleday & Co. Inc., 1966.

Jonsen, Albert, and Jeff Stryker. *The Social Impact of AIDS in the United States.* Washington, DC: National Academy Press, 1993.

Mastrantonis, George. *A New-Style Catechism on the Eastern Orthodox Faith for Adults.* St. Louis, MO: The Ologos Mission, 1969.

McNeill, John. *The Church and the Homosexual.* Boston, MA: Beacon Press, 1993.

The Rudder. Chicago, IL: The Orthodox Christian Educational Society, 1957.

Spong, John. *Rescuing the Bible From Fundamentalism.* San Francisco, CA: Harper San Francisco, 1991.

ISBN 141206825-8

9 781412 068253